Breaking
Your Horse's
Bad Habits

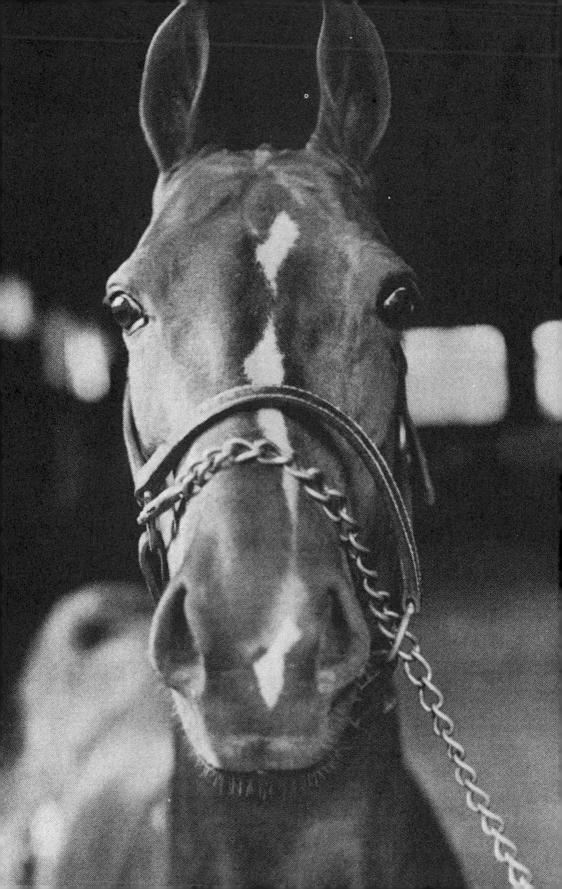

Breaking Your Horse's Bad Habits

W. Dayton Sumner

Breakthrough
PUBLICATIONS
MILLWOOD, NEW YORK 10546

This edition published 1986 by Breakthrough Publications Inc.,
Millwood, NY 10546

1st Edition 1976 by A.S. Barnes and Co., Inc.

Notice To Readers

The procedures and recommendations contained in this book should be
undertaken only with the proper professional supervision and accordingly
publisher takes no responsibility for the application of the contents of
this book including without limitation procedures, theories, and product
recommendations.

Library of Congress Cataloging in Publication Data

Sumner, W. Dayton. 1926–
    Breaking your horse's bad habits.

    Includes index
    1. Horse-training. 2. Horses—Behavior.   I. Title.
SF287.S93   636.1′08′3   74-30971
ISBN 0-914327-07-0

Printed in the United States of America
Reprinted 1993

To

SAMUEL L. ROBERTS

(1873-1938)

whose patience and caring taught
me to understand and love horses

Contents

Acknowledgments

The author expresses his appreciation to the faculty and students at the Bridle Vale School of Equitation, Mountain Lakes, N.J.; to the staff at Waseeka Farm, Ashland, Mass.; and to Dr. G. Marvin Beeman, Littleton, Colo.; for their generous assistance in obtaining the photographs that illustrate this book.

A debt of gratitude is also due to the many fine horse owners and trainers over the years who have shared their experience with me and broadened my understanding of horses and their habits.

Introduction

Like the sculptor's untouched block of marble, an untrained colt holds promise and challenge for the future. Properly and fully trained, he becomes, like the artist's dream, a joy to encounter.

But, since you have opened this book, you probably know already that there are a lot of horses who fall somewhere between those two extremes. Their training—or lack of it—has produced distinct, habitual behavior problems.

Because they are living creatures with volition of their own, horses often do things we don't want them to—or refuse to do the things we want. If their misbehavior is repeated regularly it can be labeled a vice or bad habit.

Often a nuisance and occasionally dangerous, the horse with bad habits needs special handling. And that is what this book is about.

Our first aim will be to develop a basic philosophy and a workable approach to breaking these bad habits. Beyond that, we will suggest some simple and practical techniques that even a novice horse owner can use to deal with them.

This is not a general treatise on the arts of training and riding. It is a supplement to the many fine books in that field. Our target is the horse who has already formed undesirable habits, and our focus is on ways to deal with his problems.

Opinions may differ on what constitutes good or bad habits in horses, depending on what we want of them. There's an old story, for instance, of a canny horse trader and a mare named Annuity. "Annie" was a beautiful bay. She had a finely chiseled head, small ears, dainty legs, and a lovely flowing tail. No other horse in the dealer's barn could compare with her. She was quickly sold, of course. The price was $300 and the dealer agreed to deliver her to the new owner for another $20.

Within a few days the new owners called in distress. They

couldn't get Annie to leave the barnyard. They could ride her as long as the barn was in sight, but she wouldn't go down the road. The dealer, an honorable man, agreed to take her back and refunded the $300, minus another $20 for transportation.

The whole transaction was repeated week after week. That's why the dealer named the mare Annuity. She was good for $40 a week in hauling fees as long as he could continue to sell her and buy her back again. If he had broken her bad habit, he would have lost a valuable asset.

Most equine habits can be improved considerably and many can be cured altogether. All it takes, usually, is a little common sense, some intelligent handling, and patience—lots of patience.

Success in training horses begins with understanding the animal you are dealing with. Before we can develop a sound approach to breaking bad habits we need some basic understanding of why horses act the way they do, how they learn, how they form habits, and how their natural reactions can work for or against you.

Most horse problems stem from the animal's natural fears. Insecurity is most often the common denominator. In the horse, fear is a dominant emotion because the horse is not equipped by nature to be brave. Self-preservation is the first law of nature. But with neither fang nor horn nor claw with which to defend himself, the horse is poorly equipped to preserve himself by fighting. Instead, speed and flight to evade danger are his great defenses. So nature has made him timid to protect him.

Not that the typical horse is frightened all the time. Far from it. But when fear is present, it overrides any other reaction the horse might have.

In our domestic horse, two kinds of fear—one natural and the other acquired—lead to the problem behavior we call bad habits.

The horse is naturally afraid of the unknown. Unfamiliar things cause a fear reaction which may vary anywhere from slight wariness to outright panic. When you first subject him to an unfamiliar experience, it may scare him just because it is strange.

He is equally afraid of familiar things that he knows will hurt him. The horse who has been beaten has good reason to fear the whip and the man who wields it.

Sometimes—in fact, all too often—one kind of fear is aggravated by the other. A colt spooks at something that is new to him. This brings him rough treatment or punishment for being afraid. The young horse is afraid or does not understand what is wanted of him. The human does not understand the horse's reaction. So the human punishes, and then the horse understands something.

He understands that this situation brings pain and is to be avoided in the future. Right there, a bad habit is in the making.

But if you know what makes your horse tick, you can deal with him differently and undo the mistakes that have been made in the past. Your understanding of the horse and his behavior is the first part of effective action.

With understanding, you can begin to relieve his fears and give him reasons to want to do the things you ask. Through the well-timed use of rewards and punishments, you can encourage desirable reactions and discourage unwanted behavior.

We also have trouble, at times, if we assume that the horse understands what we want him to do. We need to remember that horses do not think and reason in quite the same ways that we do. Horses do have good memories. Once they have thoroughly learned a lesson—and it takes repetition for them to learn most things—they don't easily forget.

But we are prone to think that a horse knows our wishes or that he has learned a lesson before he really has. The next time, then, it appears that the horse has forgotten or is willfully misbehaving. So you repeat the aid that the horse did not understand before. The horse becomes even more confused and the bad habits grow worse.

The late Col. Alois Podhajsky, long-time commandant of the Spanish Riding School in Vienna and one of the world's foremost horsemen, referred to his horses as his teachers. It was an apt reference, for knowledge about how to handle horses comes more than anything else from handling them. No horseman ever really completes his education, because there is always another horse somewhere that can teach him something new.

In my own experience, I've learned most from the difficult ones—the horses who presented problems for me to solve. In dealing with them I have gained new understanding of what goes on in the equine mind. The more I know about that, the better chance I have of dealing with the next horse.

In the chapters to follow that deal with handling specific habits, three points will be emphasized:

1. The horse must be taught with patience and understanding until he thoroughly accepts and understands what is asked of him.
2. Each horse is an individual. We can give general principles that work with most horses, but each horse requires a slightly different approach.
3. Taking the time to treat the horse quietly,

calmly, and gently, instead of resorting to force
and punishment, will save time in the long run
and give more lasting results.

Discipline and reprimands do have their place in this retraining
process. But they must be used at the right time and in the right
way.

This book is intended primarily as a guide to help inexperienced
horse owners find solutions to their problems. If it serves also to
remind the old-timer of some ideas he has forgotten, so much the
better.

Breaking Your Horse's Bad Habits

1
Why Horses Act the Way They Do

In the wild, horses have no bad habits—not by our definition of bad habits.

Horses acquire behavior problems as a neurotic means of coping with a basically unnatural environment. If they consistently do something we don't like, we call it a bad habit. And most of these problems grow from conflicting fears.

For instance, you ask your green colt to cross a bridge. As a result of your careful training, he wants to do what you ask. He is afraid to disobey. But what you are asking him to do also causes fear. The bridge is strange and dangerous-looking. He is afraid to cross—afraid not to.

This is the perfectly balanced fear equation. Three things can happen as a result.

You can increase his fear of not obeying. You raise your voice, dig spurs into his sides, and crack him with your crop. The fear of disobedience becomes greater than the fear of the unfamiliar. So he crosses the bridge.

The second thing that might happen is that his fear of crossing might be decreased. You dismount and lead him onto the bridge, giving him time to see that it's not as scary as it looks. He takes a timid step—then another, finds it harmless, and clops across.

In either case, you succeed by unbalancing the fear equation.

The other thing that can happen is an increase of pressure on both sides until he seeks an escape. He's too much afraid of the bridge to cross—and too much afraid of you not to. The two fears add up to panic. So he rears and throws you.

He has learned an escape route. He has, for that moment, solved his dilemma.

Once he has found an escape route from a balanced conflict equation, it will take less stress the next time to get him to try the escape that worked before. Repeat the whole episode a few times and he thoroughly learns what to do. Rearing then becomes his habitual response to any kind of stress. He has acquired a bad habit.

The fact that you promptly get up and punish him for it may not teach him to fear rearing more than the bridge. His mind may not make that connection. His brain is designed to remember the past and to deal with the present. He's not very good at predicting or imagining the future.

This does not indicate an absence of intelligence. Remember, horses are not people. They don't think the same way people do, even though we continue to expect them to. That's one of *our* bad habits, and the fallacy is as old as mankind. Primitive peoples invented sun gods, rain gods, and animal gods so they could explain the behavior of nature in terms of human thought and emotion. It is a very human tendency to believe that all animals more or less think and feel the way we do. But they don't. While there are similarities, the differences are more pronounced.

It is a mistake to say that horses are stupid. On certain rating scales, the biological scientists say that the horse's intelligence is low. A lot of horse lovers become incensed at hearing the assertion that horses are not only less intelligent than cats and dogs, but are rated dumber than rats and pigs.

These ratings are based on comparing all kinds of animals on the same kinds of tests. In nature, however, different kinds of intelligence are important to different kinds of animals.

It's a little like grading Spanish-speaking children on an IQ test based largely on English vocabulary. Vocabulary is a reasonably reliable test of a child's ability to learn—but not when the test is in a foreign language.

In the same way, it's not fair to expect a horse and a cat to do well in the same tests. Their natural needs are very different. Horses are admittedly poor at the kind of thinking it takes to catch a mouse. But they are extremely clever at the things horses need to know.

If you say that intelligence is measured by the animal's ability to get what it needs and wants—in its natural environment—the horse is far from dumb.

A knowledge of that natural environment helps us understand why horses respond and act the way they do.

Nature and evolution have given each species of animal some basic equipment for achieving its most basic needs. First, all living organisms are born with imprinted behavior patterns called instincts or instinctive drives. For an individual animal—and his whole species—to survive, it must eat, escape danger, and reproduce itself. So the most basic of instincts are hunger, security, and sex.

These are things the infant animal does not have to learn. Some very specific behavior patterns, often quite complex, are built into various animals at birth to enable them to do what nature requires of them:

— Caterpillars obey an instinctive command and spin a cocoon when it's time to begin changing into a butterfly.

— A mother salmon does not have to teach her young to swim back up the Columbia River to spawn.

— Instinctive reflexes tell skunks, porcupines, and rattlesnakes how to defend themselves from danger with the unique weapons nature has given them.

In mammals it is sometimes hard to tell which behavior patterns are truly instinctive and which are learned. Until it is weaned, the young mammal has a teacher, its mother, who in turn had a mother-teacher who learned from *its* mother—and so on for all the generations back to its origin.

So, when a colt paws at the snow to find grass underneath, we don't know whether he does it because of an inborn instinct, or because he has seen his mother do it, or perhaps because by accident he discovered for himself that this was a way to get food.

It doesn't really matter. All we need to know is that the animal has some inherited instincts which cannot be completely changed by training and many learned behavior patterns that govern the way he will respond to various situations and surroundings.

All behavior can be examined in terms of stimulus, perception, and response. You offer your horse a carrot. The sight of the carrot is a stimulus. The horse perceives something good to eat. He responds by reaching out to take the carrot. Without stimulus and perception there is no action. If there is no carrot, or if he does not recognize a carrot as something good to eat, he does not reach out. The stimulus may be internal, however. The horse's stomach is empty and he perceives that he is hungry, so he starts reaching out to find something to eat. It doesn't have to be a carrot.

If we seem to be getting away from your horse and his bad habits, it is only to be sure that we establish the importance of the basic reaction mechanisms and point out that *my* idea of how a horse should react is not necessarily the same as his.

A lot depends on perception. For instance, I am startled by a sudden noise like thunder. But if you happen to be stone deaf, you may not understand why I seem suddenly afraid. After all, as you perceive the world, nothing happened.

And that's where one of the big differences between human and equine reactions can be found. The horse is able to *sense* much that we do not, while we are able to *understand* much that he is not. What those sensations and perceptions mean to each of us may be considerably different. In dealing with horses it helps to study how they do react, and to what, rather than getting angry because they don't react the way we imagine that they should.

2
The Legacy of Nature

Let's look at the horse—at his perceptions and reactions—in the natural state. What was the horse like 10,000 years ago before man captured and tamed him? And as he exists today in the few remaining areas where horses still roam wild and free, what kind of animal is the natural horse?

Skipping the technical terminology, he is a wandering, grazing animal. His natural habitat is more or less open grasslands. He hunts no other animal, but depends on vegetation for food.

He is, however, hunted by other predatory animals. His defense against them is speed. The horse is the fastest living animal at any distance over a quarter of a mile. Some cats (the cheetah is most famous for it) and some antelopes can attain higher speeds than the horse for short distances. For 100 yards or so they may even go twice as fast as the fastest horse. But they can't maintain that speed. So, if a horse has only a 50-yard head start, there is no predator in the world that can catch him.

It is that 50-yard head start that saves his life and preserves the species. To be sure that he has that margin of safety, nature has endowed him with a fantastic warning system. His sensory receptors alert him to approaching danger and prepare him for instant action to escape.

Human beings stand on the top rung of the ladder of intelligence because of their ability to ask the question, "Why?" That is the basis for all scientific and technical progress.

The horse, on the other hand, has survived specifically because he is not able to question that way. When danger threatens, he retreats first and asks questions later. Suppose he waited to ask, "Why do you suppose those wolves are coming this way?" He would learn, too late, that they were coming to eat him up.

His sensory alarm system depends first on sight and hearing, and to a lesser extent on the sense of smell.

The way a horse sees is particularly significant. His view of the world is a lot different from ours. To begin with, he is color blind. His eye measures intensity of color as lighter or darker shades of gray. But he can't tell blue or green from a red of the same intensity.

During World War II it was found that color-blind soldiers were very good at spotting camouflaged enemy positions. Their eyes were not fooled by the artificial coloring used for concealment, and it is possible that the horse's inability to discriminate colors may help him to some extent in detecting the predators who wear spots or stripes to blend into their natural background.

But more than his lack of color perception, there is a far more significant difference in the way the horse protects himself from natural enemies with his unique type of vision.

Try this experiment. Hold up one finger about 15 inches in front of your face. Look directly at the finger. While you are seeing it in clear detail you are also aware, vaguely, of the wall across the room. You can see that the wall is there, but you can't make out much detail about it. Now, without moving your finger, shift the focus of your eyes and look at the wall beyond. It now becomes clear and detailed. And what happens to your vision of the finger? It not only blurs, but you see two finger images—one with each eye. You can see close objects or distant objects by changing the focus of the lens in your eye. But you can't see both near and far at the same time.

The horse has an unusual eyeball that makes it possible for him to keep near objects (such as the grass he is eating) and far objects on the horizon *both* in focus at the same time.

Because the need to watch for danger was so important to the wild horse, he evolved with the ability to see near and far simultaneously. But he did so partly at the expense of his ability to focus as you do by changing the shape of the lens in your eye.

He has developed, instead, a system of adjusting his focus by moving his head. People sometimes do something similar. You'll see very nearsighted people reading with the book practically touching their noses. Many others, as they enter middle age, gradually lose focusing power and have to move their heads (or the book) farther away in order to see it clearly.

As a substitute for lens focusing, the horse has what is called a ramped retina. The sensitive membrane that lines the back of

With his head down in the grazing position, the horse's unique type of vision enables him to see all of the horizon in a complete circle around him.

your eyeball and reacts to light is evenly curved so that any part of it is the same distance from the lens at the front of the eye. Not so with the horse. His retina forms an irregular curve that is distinctly nearer the lens in its lower half and farther from the lens in its upper half. Light entering the eye from below reaches the retina at a different focal length than light coming from eye level, and still different for light from above.

You can imagine what a great advantage this is to the wild horse. With his head low, as it is when he is grazing, the image of the grass he is eating enters from below and strikes the retina where it will be in focus. At the same time the image of the horizon enters from above and hits where he can focus on distance. He can thus see the grass and the wolves at the same time.

Now, try the experiment with your finger again, but this time close one eye. This way you can see both the wall and your finger with equal clarity, but you can't tell how far one is from the other.

The horse makes considerable use of monocular vision—using each eye separately. His eyes do not face squarely forward, but are placed at an angle on the sides of his head. He is able to see one "picture" with his left eye and a separate image with the other. It gives him command of the horizon in all directions at the same time. He not only sees what is in front of him, but things to the side as well. With his head up in the position he normally carries it when moving (different heights in different horses) he can't quite see all 360 degrees because his view is partly blocked by his own body. But he can see almost everything around him.

The view he gets is a wide, flat panorama, lacking perception of depth. (He probably has some appreciation of distance based on the apparent size of familiar objects.) He puts the images from each eye side by side with much the same effect you would get if you took four separate photographs of the room you are in and laid them side by side to see all four walls at once.

Without color or depth perception, the horse has some trouble differentiating detail. He sees lighter and darker shapes. But one bush looks pretty much like another. In fact, at a distance, another animal looks pretty much the same as a bush—until it moves! In this flat, colorless panorama, motion sets off the alarm system.

What does the horse do when he sees something moving toward him? He raises his head, pricks up his ears to stare and listen—to determine whether the approaching creature is friend or foe.

When he does this—after the alarm system attracts his attention—he shifts from his usual monocular vision to focus both

Most of the time a horse uses his eyes separately to see two "pictures" of the world around him. His ears also move independently, listening for danger.

When something attracts his attention, the horse focuses both eyes on the object, and his ears automatically come forward, too.

eyes forward on the same object. This gives him depth perception but cuts off his view of sides and rear. Whenever he does so, his ears automatically go forward too. He doesn't put both ears forward when he is using his eyes separately to watch things around him. Nor can he focus both eyes forward without putting his ears up. So you can always tell by watching his ears which type of vision he is using and, to some extent, what he is likely to be thinking.

With eyes and ears focused forward, his span of attention is short. He won't hold that pose for long. Again, it is nature's way of protecting him. He looks long enough to decide whether he needs to escape. But he can't afford to concentrate too long. There may be danger coming from another direction.

The action of eyes and ears together gives a clue to the way a horse constantly uses sight and hearing. His ears are the "back-up system," and they are used to supplement his vision. His hearing is very keen, and he can swivel each ear a full 180 degrees to concentrate on sounds from any direction.

If the horse's system of vision seems strange to us, we should remember that the horse doesn't think it's strange. It is the only kind of vision he has ever had and he is perfectly accustomed to it.

Where it matters to us, in dealing with horses that have habits we want to correct, is the realization that a great many bad habits are, to a large extent, visually inspired. More than anything else, it is things he has seen that have frightened him and caused the neurotic behavior that has become a bad habit.

The other primary point we need to realize is that the horse may not always be seeing what you suppose he is. It may seem that he is shying at a piece of paper on the ground beside the road. But, it might just as well be something else he sees—a hundred yards away and in another direction.

The horse's sense of smell is also part of the alarm system. He can smell other animals for a considerable distance. He is not very good at telling the smell of one animal from another. He smells something, and for a timid animal that is enough. Some veteran horsemen will tell you that a horse cannot distinguish the smell of a bear from the smell of a deer. There are certainly a lot of horses that will react to the scent of deer as if it were something to be feared. So it seems probable that scent is more important in warning the horse there is something to look out for than in telling him what it is.

There is one other significant sense that horses share with some other animals and which man has all but lost. The horse is highly sensitive to vibrations through the ground. Standing on a subway platform in New York, you may be able to feel a train coming before you see its lights down the tunnel. But your horse is much more sensitive. He can probably feel vibrations as faint as your footsteps as you walk across the yard to the barn.

We lack the scientific evidence to prove it, but there are indications that horses may also have far greater sensitivity than we do to low voltage electrical currents and perhaps even to radioactive emanations.

Just how or what they sense is less important than the fact that horses sense differently than we do. Knowing that they sense a great many stimuli we do not is vitally important to understanding and dealing with their good and bad habit patterns.

The ultimate purpose of this alarm system, and the horse's automatic fear reaction, is to move him away from danger and toward security. So that becomes the major motivating force in his life. His goal is security. It is only in a situation of security — absence of fear — that he can obey his other natural impulses to eat or reproduce. A frightened horse will neither eat nor breed. And if he won't do things as basic as these when frightened, he can hardly be expected to obey commands when he is in a state of insecurity and fear.

Perhaps you have seen the whole drama of equine psychology enacted when you went into a pasture to catch a strange horse that was contentedly grazing. At the start he was in a natural state of security. He let you approach until you were quite near. But a little before you actually reached him, he trotted away to graze some more.

Notice that he moved only fast enough and far enough to consider himself safe for the moment. When you came close again, he moved off again.

If you tried to run after him, he probably galloped away instead of trotting. But still he went just fast enough and far enough to consider himself safe for the moment, then he stopped to graze again.

That will hold true in anything you ever ask him to do. He will do whatever is required to feel safe for the moment. It's an important concept to remember.

Now suppose you maneuvered him into a corner of the pasture. He could retreat no further. So, with his escape route cut off, he turned and faced you, warily watching your approach. Did he then attack as other cornered animals might? Probably not. He watched for his chance, then dashed by you, only a few feet away depending on his speed and strength to get past. Even when cornered he would rather run than fight.

So next you chased him into a catch pen where you could close the gate. Now he was really trapped. There was no more chance to run. But, as you closed in, he still did not charge you with teeth bared and feet flailing. He kept his head away from you and kept swinging his rump toward you whichever way you moved.

That is where the horse's only effective weapon is—his hind feet. He can ward off pursuers with savage, bone-crushing kicks to the rear.

To be sure, horses also strike and bite sometimes as a defense. But this is their least effective weaponry. The horse is a defensive fighter. He attacks rarely, reluctantly, and rather clumsily.

His objective is just to reach security. Attacking seldom helps him reach that goal. In achieving what he wants most, the horse is a passive, reactive, defensive animal. And this fact is of great importance in developing an effective approach to breaking his bad habits.

3
The Effect of Domestication

If the horse is a wary animal, primarily governed by his fears, one might wonder how he could have become the willing partner of man. Why has he been praised for his courage by poets through the ages?

The origins are really part of the same defensive heritage. In nature, horses are herd animals. They live in groups. Much of their safety and security comes from this. One horse, alone on the prairie, despite his wariness and speed, may eventually be cornered and surrounded by a pack of predators such as wolves. Then, while his heels fend off some of them, others can circle and tear at his throat.

But, on the other hand, keep him with the herd and the same horse is safe. The horses form a circle of defense with too many flying heels for the wolves to penetrate.

At the head of each herd is a leader. In all the romantic stories you have read it was always a stallion, leading his band and eluding pursuers. While that was probably the normal situation, there is no hard evidence to prove that it was not sometimes a dominant mare who played the leader's role.

Just how the leadership function works in the wild is no more certain than our modern observation that there is always a "boss" in the pasture when several horses are turned out together. Why is it one of them and not another? Who knows? But the fact exists — there is a leader. There are sentries who signal the herd when danger threatens and trumpet a command to the rest to escape.

The horses that did react to command—that followed the herd—survived to find safety in the next canyon and survived to reproduce. The "loners" and independent thinkers were killed off by predators.

So evolution gave the horse, along with his wariness, the instinct to achieve security through obedience and companionship. Century upon century of domestication has accented this part of the horse's basic nature and made him amazingly amenable and trainable. Through selective breeding programs, man has also chosen the better-dispositioned horses to reproduce. The less fearful horse, under the protection of domestication, has had a better chance to survive and contribute to future generations.

It all started before the dawn of recorded history when primitive man began herding horses, originally as a food source. Archaeologists know that man had formed a hunting partnership with the dog by 6750 B.C. As man's way of life began to shift from nomadic hunting and food gathering to a more settled existence with rudimentary forms of agriculture, he began herding animals for food instead of hunting them. Sheep, goats, and pigs were probably domesticated first, followed by cattle.

It is probable that man and his dogs first pursued bands of wild horses and caught them by chasing them into a swamp, over a cliff, or into a box canyon where they could be slaughtered relatively easily. It is typical of all cultures that men tend to show mercy to the young of the species they hunt. So it is not unlikely that some of the foals were preserved and handled as pets, paving the way for later domestication and training.

Your neolithic ancestor also discovered that some of the wild horses he had caught—the mares—were worth keeping as a source of milk.

Those ancestors had already learned to use oxen as draft animals to carry burdens. It was an easy step, then, for man to use the horse's strength and greater speed to help him, particularly in hunting and in battle.

Finding the horse useful in several ways, man was willing to care for and protect his herd of horses. That gave the horse what he wanted—security. So gradually those ancient mares began teaching their foals by example that humans were not to be feared.

It has probably not been more than six thousand years since all this began—a mere moment in the time scale of evolution. It has been long enough to endow the domesticated horse with a high level of acceptance of his partnership with man, but not long enough to erase the built-in fear mechanisms. Not far below the surface there remains the original need to escape danger and seek security. It is much more pronounced in horses than have grown up on the range, away from humans.

Horses that have been near people and handled a great deal from birth seem calm, friendly and cooperative. They have, in large measure, learned to accept and depend on their human companions. And so long as nothing happens to scare them, they remain responsive and agreeable. But fear can easily upset their developed propensity for obedience and cooperation as a means to achieve security.

Fear is the ultimate imperative in the horse. If it rises to the surface, it takes command over anything else he has learned, and it produces the reactions that become bad habits.

Correcting those habits depends on quieting fears and emphasizing the comfort and security that the domesticated horse derives from satisfying his instinct to obey. To a large extent this depends on your ability to communicate with the horse effectively.

Your communication with your horse is obviously quite different from your exchange of ideas with other people. You can't talk things over with him, explain what you want, or ask questions to find out what is on his mind. You must depend on much more rudimentary signals.

A horse has essentially a two-word vocabulary. He understands "yes-no" . . . "stop-go" . . . "do-don't" . . . "good-bad" . . . "right-wrong". . . and "pleasure-pain." They are all expressions of his basic positive-negative concept. And he will perceive one or the other from every signal his senses receive from you.

I routinely teach young riders to talk to their horses, not because the words mean anything, but because the sound and the tone of voice establish a communication. Perhaps you've seen riders who approach a jump and say, "Up!" at the moment they want the horse to take off. The horse responds to the sound, but he would respond the same way if the rider said,"Down!" at that moment with the same vigor.

A horse learns early in life that soft, soothing sounds mean good, positive, reassuring things. Sharp, loud, angry sounds are negative or frightening.

The way you move around a horse also gives him messages. He has an instinctive reflex to fear sudden movement. It gives him negative input whereas slow, deliberate motion is more positive.

His sense of touch—which includes his feeling of pain from a whip and pressure from a bit—provides the most direct link of communication in almost all of your training activity. When you groom him he gets pleasant or positive signals from your touch, unless you handle him roughly in a sensitive spot such as his eyes or ears. When you ride, your seat and legs transmit messages which again may be positive or negative.

To a lesser extent, his senses of smell and taste contribute to communication. When an animal is very angry or frightened, his system releases adrenaline. It produces a subtle change in his scent. I've smelled it on a dog that has been hit by a car and on horses under extremely stressing conditions. There's no doubt that your horse will sense it, too, if you are excited, scared, or angry.

Your horse will associate each incoming signal—positive or negative—with what he is doing at that moment. If he consistently gets positive input when he relaxes and submits to your handling, he learns to adopt that attitude in order to get the pleasant sensations. On the other hand, if he regularly gets smacked and yelled at when he tries to nip, he learns to avoid doing that in order to avoid the unpleasant consequences.

Throughout this discussion of specific bad habits we will be stressing the importance of reducing your horse's feelings of stress and fear. You do that with continuing positive communications. And we will talk about correcting his mistakes with negative stimuli. In these ways you make your wants known to the horse and make use of his natural instinct to seek security.

4

Individual Differences

Now that we have established some of the reasons why horses tend to be alike in their basic motivations and reactions, it is equally important to recognize that they are all different.

While each foal is born with similar instincts, they have different levels of intelligence, aptitude, physical build, strength and nervous temperament. As he grows, the colt accumulates different experiences and acquires different habits.

The people who are most successful in training horses and correcting their bad habits are the people who approach each horse as a unique and individual problem. There is much that you do in the same way with each horse or with many horses. But when it comes down to the details, some horses will become rebellious under the same discipline that gets good results with their stablemates. Some will progress almost eagerly from lesson to lesson, and others never seem to learn anything.

An interesting example of this was a pair of colts I trained. They were both the same age, sired by the same stallion, raised side by side in the same pasture, and they were even the same color. There was probably as much reason for them to be alike as any two horses could be. But as I started to work with them, I found them really more different than alike. One was distinctly more energetic, more easily frightened, and better to handle.

After the first day or two, there was rarely a time when they both needed the same training techniques on the same day. Both reached a point of being ready to show at about the same time, but only because I had taken a different route with each of them in getting them to that point. If I had tried to use the same routine with both of them I might have succeeeded with one and failed with the other.

A common human error is trying to type horses by any means available. There are horsemen who believe black horses are smarter than chestnuts. Others will assure you that one breed (the one they own) has the best disposition. And plenty of people will tell you that all stallions require stern discipline.

Nothing could be much farther from the truth. Horses are consistent only about being inconsistent. *Some* black horses are smart; *some* individuals of each breed have good dispositions; *some* stallions need a lot of discipline.

In this enlightened age we are learning to discard racial, national, religious, and sexist stereotypes about people. In the same light there is hope that equestrians will, more and more, accept the concept of individual differences in horses.

The most obvious differences between individuals are the physical variations. It is easy enough to see that some are tall and rangy, others are short and compact or chunky. To some extent we can predict how the physical differences will affect what the individual horse can do.

Logic as well as experience tells us that the taller, Thoroughbred type is more likely to be agile over fences than some other types. More likely, yes, but far from certainly. Many horses with the perfect build for jumping are poor at it while some of the greatest jumpers in history were any shape *but* the tall, willowy stereotype.

Obviously, there are other reasons to explain why one horse seems to love to jump while another will suffer much punishment for refusing to hop over an easy obstacle.

Part of the difference is genetic. Two horses can look pretty much alike, but one is descended from a line of champions and upholds his family reputation while his look-alike comes from nondescript lines and has no more ability than his forebears.

An important reason for the individual differences is found in the intricacies of the nervous system which receives all input from outside stimuli, stores memories and experiences, and activates the muscles throughout the animal. For reasons that science does not fully understand, there are great differences in the efficiency of this system in different horses. If it were a purely electrical and mechanical system, you might say that one operates on a higher voltage than another.

Some horses run faster, jump higher, strut more proudly—and also kick more viciously—because the amount of nerve force exerted on the muscles differs greatly among individuals. They have the same structure, the same musculature; but their strength, reaction time, and agility differ greatly. That difference is what makes Olympic champions in humans as well as horses.

There are comparable differences in sensitivity to things happening around them. Some horses see better, hear better, smell more acutely, and generally react more sharply to external stimuli. There is extensive evidence that these differences have a profound bearing on the horse's disposition.

Remember that nature commands the horse to react with fear and caution when something disturbs his sense of security. The ultrasensitive horse is easily disturbed by sounds, sights, movements, and other stimuli that you may not be able to discern. Because he is always that way, he becomes predictable. He is also more sensitive to training, commands, and reassurance from his handler.

There are horses, too, that have limited or defective sensory equipment, which puts them in a more or less constant state of insecurity. A horse with small eyes, for instance, set down on either side of a prominent Roman nose, may have a tendency to poor disposition. He is wary because vision is partially blocked. Since he can't see as much, it is harder for him to feel completely secure and relaxed. He develops a sullen attitude and is likely to react unpredictably to sudden sounds and movements.

The old horse books warned that the horse that shows a lot of white around his eyes would have a bad disposition. The old books never told you why. They just said it is a sign of viciousness—and the conclusion was based on finding that many horses with this peculiarity turned out to be bad actors.

But perhaps there is a logical reason. If the iris and cornea are small, the horse has a less complete range of vision. He is insecure as a result. He has to roll his eye in its socket (and expose more of the white when he does) just to see what another horse can see without moving his eye.

If differences in ability to see affect the disposition, it is logical to suppose—and hard to prove—that variance in hearing and other senses will also make a difference. How can you tell, though, that a horse is hard of hearing and suspicious as a result?

Given their innate differences in sensory equipment and nervous reactions, horses begin accumulating experiences at birth that interact within them to mold differences in disposition, attitude, personality and temperament.

Many horses are spoiled or taught bad habits as a result of ignorant or abusive handling. Some become phobic because of a natural accident that had nothing to do with training. And there are those horses whose bad habits originated with an owner who was too timid or inexperienced to make the horse do what was asked of him.

Such a mare was brought to me for training some years ago. When the woman who owned the mare first bought her, she enjoyed long rides over the hills. Apparently deciding that some of the rides were too long, the mare would stop and abruptly turn around when she figured it was time to be starting home for dinner. If the rider tried to make her go farther, the mare would rear.

Since the rider had limited experience and the rearing scared her, she let the horse have her own way about going home. Next time out, the mare decided a little sooner to call a halt. And so it progressed with each ride getting shorter until the mare would not even go to the end of the driveway.

It was an easy enough habit to break, as we will see later when we talk about rearing.

This mare's problem was not exactly one of disposition. It was learned behavior based on experience. And since all horses have had different experiences, you can expect differences in accumulated reaction patterns.

There was a saying in the Old West: "There was never a horse that couldn't be rode, and never a rider who couldn't be throwed."

That slightly ungrammatical rhyme makes the point well enough. Every good horseman sooner or later finds some horses that he can't seem to get along with. Someone else may find the key to that horse on the first try.

The story is told that a certain Saddlebred colt in Kentucky was considered most unpromising when first started in training. The trainer was about to give up on him but turned him over to an assistant instead. Within weeks there was an amazing change. With just a slight difference in approach and handling the colt that couldn't learn anything had become sensational. The colt was Wing Commander, the greatest five-gaited show horse in history!

As we suggest approaches and methods of dealing with bad habits, bear in mind the importance of individiual differences. The horses themselves are different in their physical and nervous makeup. The experiences that created the bad habits may have been different. The handlers who are trying to bring about a cure have their differences, too.

It all argues for the use of flexible approaches in dealing with the problems. Don't expect every horse to respond the same way or at the same rate. And when one method fails to produce results, try something else. Imagination, experimentation, and innovation are of great value in figuring ways to deal with your problem horse.

If you have been trying the same technique without result, look for a way to modify it. In general, if you keep doing the same things, you will continue getting more or less the same results. If you want to change the results, try changing the things you are doing until you find a method that works.

Sometimes it is as simple as changing the signal you give a horse when you want him to do something. What may appear to be a bad habit may actually be simple confusion about what is wanted of him.

I have seen young riders on the verge of tears because a horse would not do what he has repeatedly been asked to do. That's the trouble. They literally *asked* the horse with a spoken command. The horse is willing enough. He just does not know that the syllable "trot!" means that he should begin moving his feet in a particular way.

And there is the similar problem of two confusing or conflicting commands given at the same time. The rider uses his heels to make the horse speed up and inadvertently tightens the reins at the same time, which the horse assumes is a signal to slow down.

In the final analysis, the individuality of horses is probably one of the reasons why we enjoy riding as a sport. Each horse represents a new personality and a new challenge. Because they are different, we become attached to some and dislike others. What fun would it be if all horses—or all people—were exactly alike?

5
How Horses Learn

The primary difference between a well-trained horse and one with bad habits is the difference in the things each horse has learned. Horses are not born with bad habits. They learn them. So it is helpful to understand some things about how they learn.

In all learning there are two key ingredients: experience and motivation. The animal cannot learn any way but by experience. But, unless the experience leads to a reward or punishment, nothing is learned from it.

Of all animals, only humans are capable of learning from symbolic experience. We are able to accumulate knowledge and understanding from books, lectures, films, and pictures. (In school, for instance, children are told that Columbus discovered America.) On television you have seen astronauts walking on the moon. In these ways you *learn* what the surface of the moon looks like and the student *knows* who discovered America. By transmitted symbols—words, pictures, numbers—you are able to share someone else's experience from times and places far removed from your own actual experience.

Because your brain can deal with symbols, you can also learn by deduction. You can apply one set of known factors to another situation and deduce a connection between them. You perceive that your horse is taller than you are. By direct deduction you can tell that standing on a bale of hay will make it easier for you to get on the horse.

The horse cannot think this way. He can only learn from the actual events in his own life. And he only learns to the extent that his experience is activated by motivation. If something happens that helps him gain his basic needs and desires, he learns. Otherwise, he doesn't.

The experiences that lead to learning come to him in three ways. First, he learns by imitation. In the beginning he copies his mother's actions and later he imitates other horses. If the imitative behavior gives him good feelings, provides food, relieves discomfort or insecurity, he will retain it as a learned pattern of behavior. If the feedback is negative, he will discard the activity.

He also learns by experiment or accidental discovery. Motivated by a desire for some of that "greener grass" on the other side of the fence, the colt reaches over the electric fence wire. It shocks him! Perhaps he tries again. Same result. Without learning anything about electricity, he learns that touching the fence produces an unpleasant result.

In time he will learn to associate or differentiate in varying degrees. Twice stung by the electric fence, he may from then on associate the experience with other fences and steer clear of them all. But if he is hungry enough, he may try again sometime and learn that he only gets a shock at that particular spot in that fence. By differentiation he may learn that some fences give him a shock and others do not.

Imitation provides many of the colt's early learning experiences. While his basic diet is still his mother's milk, he learns to forage for himself by copying her as she grazes.

Horses also learn by accidental discovery. If he touches an electric fence and gets a shock, he quickly learns that touching the fence produces an unpleasant result.

Association is the tendency to make a mental connection or relation between thoughts, feelings, ideas, or sensations. Differentiation is the perception of distinctions between similar objects, events and situations. Generally speaking most horses are better at associating than they are at differentiating. Their sensory systems are tuned to detecting possible dangers but not as much to discriminating one from another.

The third way a horse can accumulate learning experiences is the one most important to us. He can learn by direction. He can be taught not only to make certain moves but to rely on a trainer and to obey him.

Like the colt and the electric fence, a human baby ignores his mother's warning and touches a hot stove. He learns a painful lesson. Given a few more experiences of a similar nature, the baby begins to get the idea that mother knows best. Following her

The kind of learning that makes it possible to train horses is the animal's ability to learn from induced experience. The trainer directs the horse to move a certain way. By rewarding or punishing as necessary, she teaches the horse to obey simple commands.

instructions will prevent unpleasant consequences; ignoring them produces a penalty. So he learns to depend more on mother's directive than on the apparent situation.

That kind of learning is what makes it possible to train horses. The trainer induces experiences. If he is a good trainer, positive response by the horse brings consistent reward; negative responses consistently produce correction. The more consistent the trainer is, the more readily the horse will learn. And the more he learns to accept the trainer's direction, the more he will depend on the trainer over his natural instincts. His increasing dependence then makes it harder for him to disobey.

The one thing a horse wants more than anything else—his most basic motivation—is to be free of fear. He constantly seeks a state of emotional security. Most domesticated horses achieve this most of the time. It is only when they become insecure that they develop bad habits. Much of the horse's security, in fact, comes from learning to depend on his trainer's directives. With this motivation he quite readily and willingly learns to perform tasks because his experience tells him they lead away from harm and toward security.

Several factors influence how quickly and thoroughly a horse (or a human) will learn a particular lesson and how well he will retain what he has learned. Apart from the differences in individuals we have already discussed, learning is affected by primacy, frequency, recency, and vividness of the learning experience.

A first encounter with a particular set of circumstances tends to be remembered more sharply than subsequent similar experiences. Most people, for instance, remember their first horseback ride much more clearly than their twenty-third or their three hundred and thirteenth.

Experiences that are repeated frequently are retained better than things done only a few times. Something done most recently will be clearer in the memory than earlier experiences, until some other event replaces it as the most recent.

The first, most frequent, and latest experiences are remembered because they are intense or vivid. Unusual significance or emotional impact can also intensify an isolated experience so that it stands out permanently in your memory. We remember dramatic moments longer than routine ones. The same is true of horses.

There is relatively recent research, in fact, that strongly suggests that nothing in our lives is ever completely forgotten. It merely becomes too remote to be called to consciousness. But if the right spot on the brain is stimulated with an electric probe, you may suddenly recall a long-"forgotten" experience—the words to an old song, for instance—and you will experience the same emotions you did when you heard it long ago. It is all stored somewhere in the brain, waiting for later experience to call it up or modify it. If this is the way the human brain works, there is no reason to suppose than an equine brain, operating at its own level of intelligence, does not also work the same way. It is probable that a horse's old experiences are also on tap and will influence his behavior in later situations.

While you may have vivid conscious memories of pleasant and exciting experiences, almost all of a horse's most intense recollections are negative. He remembers well anything that hurt or scared him particularly badly—even if it only happened once a long time ago. And since he does have that propensity, it is quite likely that when a similar situation presents itself he will react to his remembered fear and do something violent. This will bring negative consequences again and therefore reinforce the original terror. Example: The horse was once beaten by a sadistic groom who smelled strongly of garlic. Long afterward a stranger approaches who happens to have the same strong smell of garlic on his breath. The odor awakens the horse's old memory and he becomes fractious. So he is disciplined for his unusual behavior and he becomes more sure than ever that people who smell of garlic are dangerous.

In that way a horse's traumas tend to be self-reinforcing which makes them dominant and hard to erase. They are the foundation of most of his bad habits. So in setting out to correct them, you have your work cut out for you.

However, you have a great deal of control over the learning environment and the input the horse receives. You can exclude, at least temporarily, many negative stimuli and extraneous distractions until repetition and direction give the horse enough confidence in you to offset his natural fears.

It is rather like building a bank account with small deposits until you have a large enough balance to make a large withdrawal. You ask your horse to do simple things over and over again, rewarding him as he does so. Eventually you will be able to ask him for something more difficult and he will accept it.

Motivation is what makes an animal move and do things. It may be either positive or negative. A horse will move toward food when he is hungry (positive incentive) and away from danger or discomfort (negative). When he is neither hungry nor afraid—when he has no immediate motivation—he stands still.

In the horse, positive motivation tends to produce slower, calmer movement than negative motivation. A hungry horse will walk or trot to the barn if you call him at feeding time. But a frightened horse will react with faster, more violent movement, bolting at top speed away from something that frightens him.

While this seems to suggest that negative incentives are more potent than positive ones, it does not follow that horses learn faster from punishment than from reward.

In work with a variety of animals, B. F. Skinner, a leading authority in behavioral research, found that punishment is less effective in behavioral control than positive (rewarding) reinforcement. Moreover, in a series of experiments with different species he demonstrated that all kinds of animals learn in much the same way. The learning curves for one species of animal cannot be distinguished from the graphs for another animal.

In the learning process, results seem to come in irregular bursts rather than by steady improvement. Psychologists speak of "learning plateaus." A lesson may be repeated for a number of days with no apparent improvement. Each day the horse seems to have forgotten what you painstakingly taught him the day before. Then, suddenly, one day he remembers and continues day after day at a new level until something clicks again inside and he steps up to the next level or plateau. This is the normal pattern of learning.

I have never trained a young horse that did not show me at least one plateau rather dramatically. When I first start riding a colt, he seems awkward. He has to learn how to balance himself with my weight on his back. He goes along this way for a time. Then suddenly, one day there's a different feeling under me. The colt seems to come to himself. He comes up into the bridle, moves with confidence, and clearly shows me that he's ready to learn other things. It has never failed, and it always happens abruptly.

Skinner also demonstrated that learning is greatly affected by whether or not the desired response is natural and appropriate for the animal. Pigeons, for instance, can easily be taught to peck at a certain symbol to get food. It is practically impossible, though, to teach them to peck the same symbol to avoid getting an electric shock. They easily learn to go to the opposite end of the cage to avoid the shock. Pecking is obviously an "appropriate" way for a pigeon to get food but not very "appropriate" for avoiding unpleasantness. For that, retreating is the apt response.

Applying the same logic to horses, you can first expect difficulty in teaching a horse to do something that is completely unnatural to him. However, by selection of the right or "appropriate" stimulus you can usually get a desired response that is within the range of natural equine actions. This suggests again the value of using a flexible approach. If the method you have been using is not working, consider it "inappropriate" and try another. If punishing the horse for his misdeeds does not work, consider the use of a positive incentive instead, and vice versa.

The things we know about how horses learn suggest some basic points on how to teach them better.

First, don't try to teach two things at the same time. Avoid confusion. The simpler the task, the more readily it is learned. If your horse has a bad habit you want to break, work on that alone until he responds. Don't mix it in with teaching him other things.

Next, be consistent. Use the same signal each time you ask for a certain response. Provide a similar reward each time the horse responds; give him the same kind of reprimand when he doesn't.

Finally, be distinct and definite about the signals you use. Don't make the horse guess whether your heel is asking him to move, or whether your foot is just swinging a little in the stirrup.

Habit is the end result of learning. A learned response to a given signal is repeated and reinforced until it becomes the horse's customary reaction. When he reaches the point where he automatically responds in a certain way to a given stimulus, he can be said to have established a habit. If this action is what we want, we call it a good habit. When his learned behavior involves undesirable actions we label them bad habits and look for ways to change them.

6
How Habits Are Formed

Horses are very much creatures of habit. Once they learn a routine that leads to security feelings, they are most comfortable repeating it. Your grandparents may remember the milk-wagon horse who knew all the stops on the milkman's route. He did not need to be driven at all. He knew when to start and where to stop. The routine had become a habit, and as long as he was not asked to deviate from that routine he was comfortable.

Saying that horses are creatures of habit is another way of saying that they are inclined to follow a course of learned behavior as long as it gets them what they want—or until something happens to prevent them from doing it. Similarly, the more times a horse gets what he wants by escaping a stress situation with an undesirable reaction, the more he reinforces the habit—and the harder it may be to break it.

While a habit is a response pattern that is originally learned, it is important to realize that habits become semi-voluntary. That is, while the response can be controlled by a conscious act of will, it is usually so nearly automatic that the habitual reaction will always follow the stimulus unless something happens to stop it.

If the things a horse has learned are good habits, and they are continually reinforced, the horse is likely to spend his whole life being a dependable and useful citizen. It is his semi-automatic habit to do what is asked of him.

Most horses, in fact, have remarkably good memories. Once they learn something, even if they don't encounter the same situation again for years, they will usually remember and respond again as they did before.

But this learning-memory factor works the same way with

undesirable behavior. While the memory of a bad experience tends to fade in time if it is not repeated, time alone will rarely erase an established reaction pattern. As an example, suppose a colt was badly frightened when first hitched to a breaking cart. After several unsuccessful attempts at driving during which he ran away, broke harnesses, and demolished buggies, his owner gave up and stopped trying to teach him to drive. Three or four years later a new owner, not knowing about the earlier trauma, tries to hook him. The horse remembers every detail of his panic and reacts exactly as he did before.

If the new owner wants to drive the horse, he will have to go through a retraining program to calm the horse's fears and then, starting from the beginning, prepare him to drive.

We have advanced the proposition that bad habits—or neurotic responses—generally stem from a stress situation.

One stress situation is the kind we have already noted in which the horse is naturally afraid to do something that is asked of him. He has also learned to depend on his trainer's directives and feels insecure about not doing what his handler commands. If the fear on both sides is *not* equal, he will move in the direction of least fear. If the task is really simple and his confidence in the trainer is great, he will hesitate and then do what is asked of him. On the other hand, if his fear is great and his confidence in the trainer is less, he will simply refuse. It is where the two forces are *balanced* that he attempts an alternate escape.

This might seem to suggest that the way to cope with all situations is to make the horse so much afraid of the trainer that any other threat seems small by comparison. Unfortunately, there are some trainers who operate on that basis. They do, in fact, get results of a kind. But the results are generally not desirable.

The heavy-handed trainer whose whip is the solution to all problems creates a sense of apprehension in the horse at all times. The animal lives in constant fear, waiting for the next beating. The pervading feeling makes the horse more and more fearful of everything. The stress builds and builds. The trainer must use more and more abuse to get his way until the horse either becomes a totally unmanageable outlaw, or until his spirit is broken completely. It is quite literally like a nervous breakdown. The horse perceives his situation as so hopeless that he gives up. The resulting shadow of a horse is never willingly cooperative and no joy to own.

Other stress situations that lead to bad habits are not directly based on fear. Possibly the most common is the horse who is a little too well fed and not exercised enough. He has an abundance of natural energy and no normal outlet for it. Inability to use up that energy produces a kind of insecurity, too. So he invents ways to discharge the surplus vigor.

The resulting habits are not always cured by simply putting the horse to work more regularly. I recall a three-year-old Thoroughbred stud whose promising career on the track was interrupted when he suffered a fall and dislocated his stifle. He was laid up a long time, and the enforced inactivity gave him increasingly nasty habits. By the time he was sound enough to go back to work he was really unmanageable. After several dangerous incidents he was ruled off the track completely. The last time I heard, he was terrorizing grooms and jockeys on half-mile tracks in Mexico. He was a victim of habits acquired from stresses, and they were never broken.

Perhaps there is another kind of balanced equation. Consider the horse that seems to want nothing but to be fed and left alone. For him, this is complete security. Either he has never had the kind of training that would give him respect or confidence in a trainer or he has been spoiled by a lack of necessary discipline. The result, when he is taken out to work, is that nothing you ask of him provides a suitable replacement for the security of being left alone. There is no fear—nor stress, really. But no motivation either, except to get back to the barn. These are the horses that develop any number of habits to avoid working. Their "laziness" is not necessarily incurable. But, as a type, they require some handling that is a little different, unlike the handling for those that learned bad habits to escape fear or stress.

This pattern is typical of many riding-school horses that are handled by many different people. With so many different riders, most of whom have limited skill, it is just too confusing for a horse to learn what each one wants. He gets little emotional reward for his efforts and develops a typically lazy attitude toward life.

The solution in any of these cases usually lies in complete retraining. The horse must first unlearn the bad habit and then learn to substitute a good one. Quite often you can only guess at how the bad habit got started. You may never completely reconstruct the events. But you can begin with the assumption that there was a point where his fear of not doing a task was equal to his fear of doing it. There was a point where both fears were strong enough to spark a neurotic escape mechanism. Since you don't know what that point was, you need to start at the beginning of any particular pattern of activity to relieve its stresses and substitute rewards and security.

Some behavioral problems you will encounter are not true habits. Some are direct, reflex responses to a specific stimulus. Unlike a habit, a reflex is not learned and is completely automatic. All animals have reflexes to withdraw from pain, for instance. If you touch a hot stove, reflex action will pull your hand away from it before you even feel the pain consciously. A nerve impulse goes to the muscles without traveling to the brain first. Your eyelid also operates on reflex. Try as you may by force of will to hold the lid open, you can't touch your eyeball with your finger. You have to hold the lid open with one hand in order to put drops in your eye.

Reflexes are nature's automatic protective devices. Since they are not learned, they can't be unlearned. You can't cure them. You can only modify and control them.

In later chapters we will be discussing specific remedies for a number of habit and behavior problems. With some of them, such as bucking, rearing, halter pulling and kicking, for instance, it is easy to picture how such a habit could develop as an escape or defense in a stressing situation. But what gratification does a horse get out of a habit like cribbing? That's harder to figure.

But then, if you know someone who habitually bites his fingernails you may be equally bewildered about what satisfaction he gets from it. That person, in fact, would undoubtedly have difficulty explaining.

Let's assume that all behavior produces some kind of reward. Assume further that this reward contributes in some way to the essential feeling of security. Then the answer to some strange habits may not be so hard to find. In whatever way the habit got started, it now has become so much a part of the individual that the routine of doing it is in itself a source of security. In that sense, it has become a part of the individual's personality. Without it he feels insecure. It leaves a vacuum that must be filled with some other behavior as a substitute. And this is as true with horses as it is with people.

There is a danger in generalizations, because every "rule" has its notable exceptions. But in dealing with the causes and cures of habits there are some useful axioms that tend to hold true much of the time:

1. Stress is the most usual cause for neurotic escape behavior.
2. An escape that succeeds is likely to be repeated.
3. Repeated behavior forms a learning pattern, and reinforcement solidifies it as a habit.
4. Before a habit can be broken, its component parts must be unlearned.

5. A new response must be repeated and reinforced until it is learned and becomes a habit.

7
How Habits Are Changed

We have compared a bad habit to a balanced equation, saying that when a horse's motivation for doing a task is equaled by his motivation for not doing it, there is a conflict or stress that makes him seek escape.

In the axioms of habit formation, this stress causes the first attempt at escape; an escape that succeeds is repeated; repetition becomes habit; and habits produce semi-voluntary actions that will continue until something is done to change or prevent them.

In broad terms, then, there are three things you can do to change this chain of events. You can reduce the horse's reason (usually fear) for not wanting to do what you ask. You can increase his motivation or confidence in doing what you ask. And you can make it more difficult for him to escape from the situation by preventing his chosen escape route.

Reducing Fear

If your horse is afraid of something you ask him to do because it is unfamiliar, it is relatively easy, usually, to unbalance the equation in the right direction. It is perfectly natural for the horse to fear situations that are new to him. But, by the simple expedient of making the unfamiliar more familiar you can often get the horse to accept what you ask of him. All you have to do is expose him to these things in an atmosphere free of stress.

For instance, a young horse is likely to get upset the first time you ask him to load in a trailer. The trailer is a large, strange, ominous sight. But if you prepare him for travel by parking the trailer in his pasture for a few days, with the tailgate open, he will have a chance to investigate it and get used to it. If you leave feed or hay in it and let nature take its course, a nosy colt will quite likely teach himself to load.

Wherever unfamiliarity is the cause of the horse's reluctance, the obvious solution is to give him an opportunity to get acquainted with the situation before you ask him to approach it.

Bad habits, though, are more often the result of some situation or stimulus which gave the horse a reason to fear it. Something happened, in other words, to hurt or frighten him, and he naturally wants to prevent that from happening again.

Whatever that frightening past experience was, it did not happen in a vacuum. It was surrounded by a pattern of events. He is likely to associate his bad experience with that whole pattern, not just parts of it that caused him discomfort. If so, he will react negatively to any part of it.

If a horse has been ineptly handled, for instance, in his training for stock horse classes, and has been hurt by rough hands on the reins yanking him to make his sliding stops, he is likely to show reluctance and a sour attitude about any part of his individual work. Similarly, many horses that have been schooled for barrel racing or pole bending become highly excited any time they are taken into an arena—even when there are no poles or barrels set up. They identify the general surroundings with a set of specific past experiences.

I once had a Thoroughbred hunter who had been raced as a colt. In the show ring—either on the flat or over jumps—he was quiet and showed impeccable manners. But one time we went to a show that was being held on a race track. As soon as he set foot on the track and saw the once familiar surroundings, a change came over him. His head and ears came up. There was a sudden tense anticipation in his step. And during the whole show all he wanted to do was run.

These established memories are an integral part of your horse's current reactions. If you want to change the way your horse behaves—to break his bad habit—it is usually helpful to break up these associative patterns and let him learn new reactions to the separate parts of the pattern one at a time.

Most of the things we ask a horse to do are not single tasks but a composite of a number of subtasks. If you tack your horse up to go for a ride you are really expecting him to accept a number of related but separate things: he must accept a bridle on his head and a bit in his mouth; he is asked to carry a saddle on his back with a girth snugged up around his barrel; he must accept another creature getting on his back; he is supposed to adjust his own balance to move correctly while compensating for the weight of a rider. Beyond that, you ask him to respond to signals given through the bit, your voice, your legs and your whip. He must execute different gaits on command, stop, negotiate obstacles (both physical and mental) and perhaps keep pace with your companion's horse.

All of these are subtasks. They add up to a single pattern. But each separate subtask has a potential for creating stress of one kind or another. So a little wariness about one part of the job added to a little discomfort from the tack, perhaps, and a little misunderstanding about what the rider wants, can add up to a distinctly uneasy feeling. If that develops, it takes very little more stress to create the balanced equation that produces unwanted behavior. Asking him to cross an unfamiliar bridge may be the trigger that sets off violent refusal. But it is quite possible this is just the last straw. The strange bridge would not create a problem if he were secure about the other things.

So the constructive approach to discouraging bad habits is to deal with the various subtasks in the pattern and relieve their potential for stress.

Let's go back to the example of the colt who was badly frightened when first hooked to a breaking cart and see how it might help to begin over again with him.

He is afraid of a patterned situation. We do not know which elements in the pattern bother him the most. Perhaps they all do. His fear doesn't show on the surface when you put the harness on—but a little of it may be there. It is still not apparent if you drive him in long lines. He may even suppress it if you ask him to pull a drag. But any or all of these subtasks may be contributing to his fear. He is completely primed, and when you hook him to the cart, he explodes.

But now the trainer tries something else. One day he just puts the harness on—quietly and gently. He talks to the horse, pats him, and perhaps gives him a treat to eat. Then he quietly removes the harness and puts the horse back in his stall.

Next day the same thing. And the next. By the end of the week, the horse is thinking, "This isn't bad at all."

After that he is hardly perturbed when the trainer takes him out

with the harness on and lunges him for a little while. A few days of
this and the horse is readily accepting the idea that wearing
harness and moving around in it is not necessarily going to lead to
something dreadful. Each time he does the subtasks and gets
rewards instead of trauma he gets positive reinforcement for a
new pattern of responses.

Gradually the trainer adds new subtasks—one at a time. First,
line driving, later the drag or "Indian poles." And each time
something new is added and the horse accepts it, he goes back to
the barn. The trainer knows that an extra week or two of work now
can pay off with years of usefulness later.

Finally, when all the preliminary subtasks have become part of
a positive habit pattern that the horse is comfortable with, the
actual hooking to a cart is no longer the detonator that sets off the
powder keg—because the powder keg is empty.

Still, the trainer makes the first try at the cart a brief one. With
the help of an assistant, he hooks the horse, leads him just a few
yards in a straight line. He avoids making any turns because the
horse might be startled if his hind leg touches a shaft of the cart.
Without even getting into the driver's seat this time, the trainer
stops the horse, unhooks him again, and puts him away. Hooking
is one subtask; driving is another.

If there were an easier, simpler way—a short cut or "instant"
solution—I would tell you so. But as long as bad habits are learned
by repetition of stress-producing situations, they must be unlearned by comparable repetition of good subhabits, constantly
reinforced with the reward of security to displace fear. The only
difference, perhaps, is that it takes more patience and repetition
first to undo the negative response and then to establish a new
one.

Increasing Confidence

The progress you make in the direction of reducing or removing
the horse's fear of doing things you ask is usually complemented
by a growing confidence in you. The more you handle him, calm
him, reassure him, correct him, reward him, the more he will
learn to feel safe in doing what you ask of him, and the more
reluctant he will be to disobey.

This kind of progress takes place whether you are working
directly on a bad habit or not. Every contact you have with a horse
adds or subtracts from the balance in your "confidence account"
with him.

A handler who is inconsistent in the way he handles a horse is like a person who puts money in the bank one day and draws it out the next. He doesn't earn interest that way, and his balance never gets much larger.

Being consistent is not a matter of always doing the same things with a horse. It is a question of giving similar signals each time you want a certain response. Equally important, it means responding to the horse in the same way whenever he does certain things. For instance, a horse that is inclined to nip will get over it sooner if he is reprimanded *every* time he does it than if he is ignored sometimes and sharply punished other times.

Too much reliance on a single routine may actually have undesirable results. If you take a horse into the same training ring every day, and put him through exactly the same paces, in the same order every day, he will begin to anticipate the routine more than he responds to your commands. Aside from the fact that horses seem to get bored, or sour, with too much of the same schooling, they quickly learn to expect the next move. Instead of relying on your signals, they want to complete their routine because they have learned that this will earn them the reward of returning to the barn. By working in different places and varying the sequence of exercises, while keeping your methods consistent, you build the horse's eagerness, interest, and confidence in you.

Forcing His Acceptance

Some trainers believe there is great value in a more dramatic method of teaching a horse to accept your handling. They use a casting harness to throw the horse to the ground, tie him up, and leave him helpless for a while. When the horse has stopped struggling, they return and rub him all over briskly with a sack or towel before releasing him. Although the system does undoubtedly show a stubborn horse who is boss, it is not a technique recommended for inexperienced handlers. If the horse needs this treatment, it's best to put him in the hands of a competent professional for a while.

There is a somewhat milder version of the same idea, however. For this you need about twenty feet of stout rope and a hobble strap. (The strap should be two inches wide and long enough to buckle around the horse's ankle. It should have a stout buckle and a D-ring, and it is best if the strap is covered with sheepskin.

Buckle the strap around one hind pastern. Double your rope

and tie one end loosely around the horse's neck just in front of his shoulders. Use a nonslip knot. Pass the other end of the rope through the D-ring on the hobble strap and draw it up tight so the horse cannot put that foot on the ground. Tie the rope securely and leave the horse alone. He will struggle until he learns that he can't put that foot down. Give him time to absorb that thoroughly, then approach him calmly, sack him out thoroughly, going all over him and talking to him. Then release him when he seems completely docile about your movements.

In my own opinion, this is a short-cut method and not as desirable as the slower approaches to winning a horse's confidence. There are times when it may be useful. But it can backfire and make some horses more fearful than they were before. When other methods have failed, it is a possible solution with some horses. I would certainly not advise trying it with every horse that gives you minor problems.

Rewards and Punishment

It seems obvious to say that the basis of all training is to reward the animal when he does the right things and reprimand or punish him when he doesn't. But that is really what it is all about. What may not be so obvious is what constitutes an appropriate reward or punishment.

In general, the rewards available to a trainer are more subtle and less dramatic in their effect than the punishments he can use. Contrary to popular belief, carrots, sugar, and other edible treats are not among the more effective rewards available to you. They have their place, but they won't overcome a horse's fears. If I give a horse a lump of sugar when he is feeling secure, it helps him associate his good feelings with me. But I have never seen a horse that could be coaxed to do something he really fears by offering him a carrot. More often, I have seen a horse refuse or spit out the treat if it is offered when he is upset.

There is, surprisingly, a greater reward value in a gentle hand, a soothing voice, and an intangible vibration of confidence. In nature, where the horse's very survival depended on living in a herd, he developed an instinct for company. He is innately more comfortable being with other living creatures—including humans—than being alone. And in the same environment, evolution sharpened his ability to sense the feelings of other animals around him. If a member of the herd caught sight of an approaching marauder, the others tuned in on his fear almost immediately.

The domesticated horse is almost as acute as his wild ancestor in sensing these imperceptible warnings. If there is a difference in their sensitivity, it is probably only because the stable-raised horse has been exposed to people and their doings long enough to learn they generally mean no harm.

In the West, a century ago, when wild mustangs were captured, they were far more skittish and fearful than horses raised around people. But in spite of that, they were surprisingly easy to train. Like domesticated horses, they soon transferred their dependence to their human handlers. They were used to following the leader of the herd. It was natural for them to accept and follow orders. So their instinct helped them adjust to a new kind of leadership.

The one thing that you probably cannot do is fool the horse about how you are feeling. He has an ability to sense whether you are angry and afraid, or relaxed and confident. This is one of the reasons why I have given up trying to work with most horses when my temper is frayed and ragged. I may have enough control to keep myself from taking out my frustrations by hitting a horse when he doesn't deserve it. But I can't prevent him from feeling that I am upset, and that prevents me from rewarding him with the positive feelings he should be receiving from me.

At the same time, the horse's "sixth sense"—which is really an ability to read imperceptible signals with his conventional senses—also enables a horse to tell the difference between a good-natured swat on the rump when you are pleased and a corrective slap in the same place when you are not. The difference is in your manner, not in the force of the blow.

Punishments, on the other hand, are more distinct than rewards and provoke a sharper reaction. It may take days before a horse responds to soothing words but an angry shout gets an immediate reaction.

Anything that you can do to hurt or frighten a horse can be used as a punishment. Most trainers use the suggestion or threat of punishment far more than actual chastisement. Teaching a colt to lunge, for instance, they let him see the lunge whip—and perhaps crack it occasionally—to urge him along. They rarely need to hit him with it.

Your voice is probably your most useful training aid. You always have it with you, you can use it when both hands are occupied, and you can tune it to apply either reward or punishment as you need it.

The whip, however, is a basic piece of equipment and it is appropriate to review its use. We do not advocate abuse or cruelty. It is neither necessary nor effective. But it is chiefly in romantic fiction that horses are trained entirely with rewards and kindness. The horse is bigger than you are. He is stronger. Without a whip, you would have to find some other way to communicate disapproval, to direct his responses, or to command his attention. For some centuries the whip has been basic because it serves a valid and useful purpose.

There is an old rule on how to use it, though: "Hit him seldom...hit him hard...hit him quick."

The use of the whip tells the horse, "What you are doing right now is wrong. When you do this, pain will result." Sometimes you can communicate this message without actually using the whip. But there are times when nothing else will do the job as well.

The right time to use a whip on a horse is when you want him to understand he is doing something wrong. When that time comes, make sure that you do it smartly enough for the horse to get the message clearly. Don't be halfhearted about it. One good crack now may save you the need of giving him a half a dozen more later on. But using the whip too often—especially tapping him frequently with it—leads him to suppose that everything he does is wrong. If he begins to find that he gets a sting no matter what he does, it no longer has any meaning to him.

Timing is particularly important. As the rule says, hit him quickly when he does something wrong. If you hit him after he stops, he will think you hit him for stopping, not for what he did.

I have known a few horses whose habits were so deeply ingrained or whose temperaments were so rebellious that they were quite impervious to any amount of whipping. They either did not respond at all or fought back when punished with a whip. Without exception, these horses should be considered dangerous. Their retraining, if any, should be in the hands of a competent professional. There may be ways to deal with some of them, but in general a horse that is too neurotic to respond to normal methods of punishment is a poor bet.

When you are riding, a sharp tug on the reins or a jab with your heel may be used as a mild form of correction or instruction. An inexperienced rider may tend to do either of these things—or both at once—unintentionally. If he does, the horse may be understandably confused. Until a rider has good control of his legs he is not ready to begin trying to break bad habits.

Rewards, in the form of reassurances that give the horse security feelings, are useful in getting the horse to do what you want him to. Punishments, though, are more useful in stopping him from doing what you don't want.

Preventing Escape Behavior

In the fear equation, the horse invents a neurotic escape because, for him, it is the easy way out of a pair of stresses he can't handle. What he does instead may seem to us a great deal more difficult than the simple task asked of him. But the horse doesn't see it that way. He finds it easier, and he is the one we have to deal with.

Now, what would happen if his regular escape route were made more difficult or cut off altogether? He has to make a new choice: either do what he refused originally or find a different way to escape.

In managing bad habits you need appropriate ways of restraining and controlling the horse to prevent his undesirable behavior. Several simple methods are available.

In most cases, if you can control a horses's head you can control the whole horse. On the other hand, if he feels his head is free, he will fight any other kind of restraint until something gives.

It is wise to remember that restraints can sometimes stir up greater reaction than the behavior you are trying to control. It is not necessary to truss the horse up like a Christmas turkey to trim him, for instance, if simply holding one ear and twisting it a little will do the job.

Twisting an ear is one of the simple restraints. Another you may need when the vet has to work on the horse's head is to stand under the horse's neck, facing forward, with your hips against the horse's chest. Reach up on both sides of his neck to hold both his ears at once. In this position, the horse can't strike you because you are too close. And if he rears, he may lift you off your feet, but he can't get away from you.

Another variation, sometimes useful for trimming, is to stand on one side of his head (facing his rear). Reach across and hold the opposite ear so you can clamp his nose between your elbow and your side. This leaves one hand free to soothe the horse, hold the other ear, or do whatever it is you are restraining the horse for.

A lot of simple procedures from mounting to administering medicine become a lot easier through the simple expedient of having an assistant hold one of the horse's front feet off the

A safe way to restrain a horse when it is necessary to give him medicine. By standing close under the horse's neck and grasping both of the horse's ears, the handler is able to hold the horse's head but is too close for the horse to strike. If the horse rears, he may lift you off your feet, but he can't get away.

ground. It won't absolutely prevent the horse from kicking—some horses can balance on two diagonally opposed legs and lash out with the other hind foot. But holding one foot up often helps.

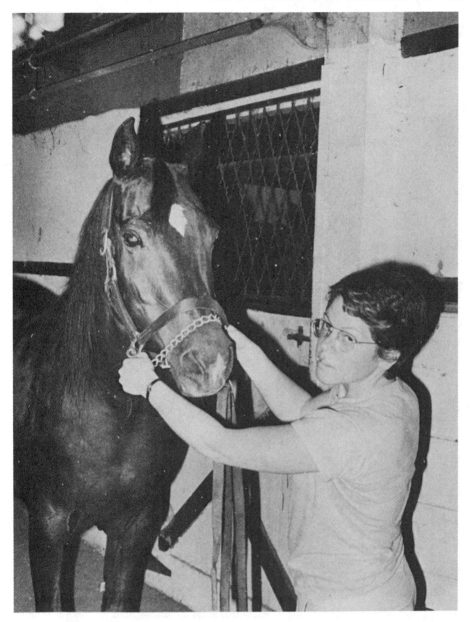

For a horse that needs to be restrained or held back, the most usual arrangement is to pass the chain end of a lead shank through the halter ring on the near side, over his nose, and snap it to the ring on the other side.

One of the most regularly useful items is a lead shank with chain and snap. There are several ways to use it, depending on the problem you are dealing with.

Placing the chain over the horse's nose is a more effective control than trying to hold back an eager horse by just pulling on the halter.

For a horse that needs to be restrained or held back, the most usual arrangement is to pass the end of the chain through the lower halter ring on the near side, carry it over his nose, and snap it in the ring on the other side.

With this arrangement, the chain is a more effective control than trying to hold back an eager horse with just your own strength pulling on the halter. If the horse still tries to outpull you, a sharp

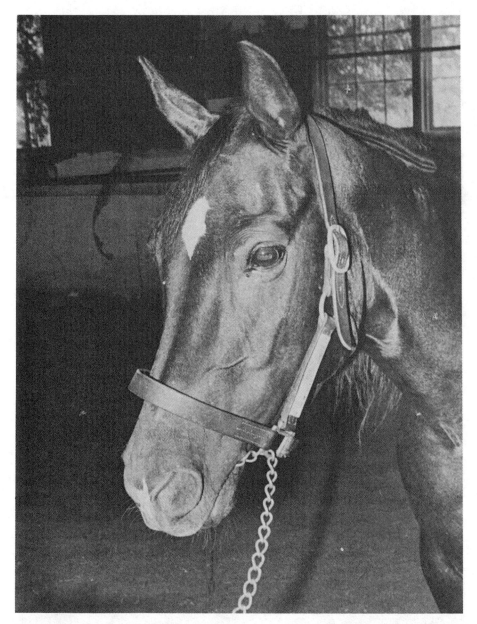

Passing the chain through the horse's mouth gives you the control you would have with a bit in his mouth.

jerk on the shank usually gets his attention and brings him back under control.

A variation of this arrangement is to pass the chain through the near halter ring, then through the horse's mouth (instead of over his nose) to snap on the other side. In this way the chain gives you the control you would have with a bit in his mouth.

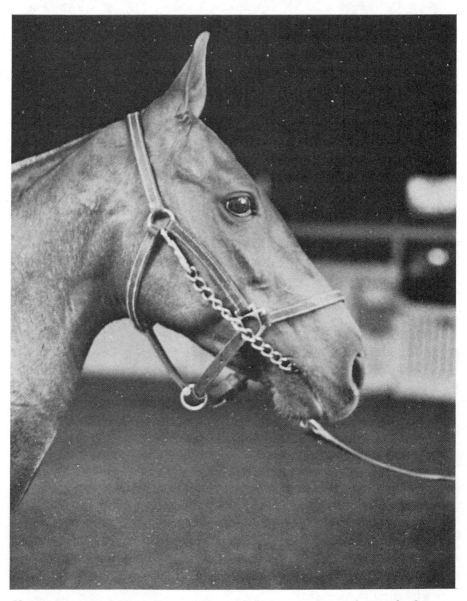

Using the upper halter ring on either side increases the mechanical advantage and provides a stronger restraint.

Effective in some cases where you need rather stringent restraint is passing the chain through the halter ring, then across the gum under his upper lip, again snapping to the opposite halter ring. This applies sharp pressure to a sensitive spot.

Any of these methods help to control horses whose evasive movement is forward. But they work against you with the horse who won't move forward when you want him to—such as the horse who won't load in a trailer.

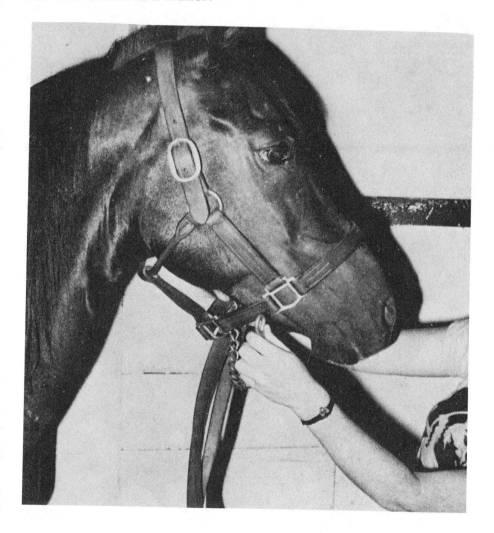

For the horse that won't move forward it is often more effective to fasten the chain under the horse's jaw instead of over his nose.

For these cases you can pass the chain shank through the near halter ring, then *under* the horse's jaw, and snap it to the opposite ring. The horse will tend to move away from the pressure point which is now behind his nose, not in front of it.

Next to the chain shank the most generally useful restraint is the twitch (sometimes called a "twister"). There are several types. The simplest consists of a handle and a loop of rope. You

A basic piece of equipment in any stable is a twitch. This is a commercial version with a chain loop. A homemade handle with rope loop may be used instead.

can make one by drilling a hole through one end of a length of discarded broomstick. Thread an eighteen-inch length of sash cord or light rope through the hole and tie the ends of the rope together with a secure square knot.

To use it, put one hand through the loop in the twitch. Grasp the horse's upper lip gently but firmly and move the loop off your hand and around the lip. As you do so, begin twisting the handle with your other hand to tighten the loop around the horse's nose. Twist it tight.

The discomfort it causes the horse will distract his attention from other things, and most horses will stand quite still while restrained this way. If he does not stand still enough, twist the loop a little tighter. *Don't* pull on the twitch as it may easily slip off his nose. Instead, twist.

Be careful also not to lose your grip on the handle if the horse moves suddenly. He can repay your attentions with a nasty whack on the head from the handle of the twitch.

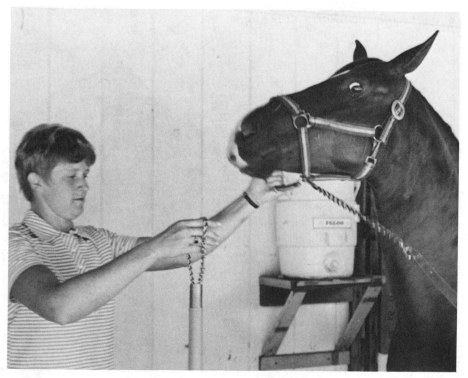

Approaching the horse calmly, the handler hangs the twitch over one hand leaving the fingers free to grasp the horse's upper lip.

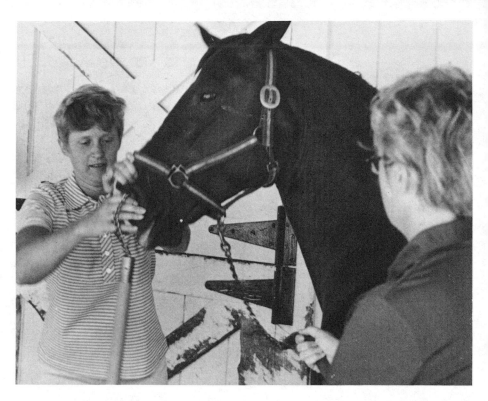

Calming the horse as much as possible, the handler gets a firm hold on the upper lip and lets the twitch slip off the hand.

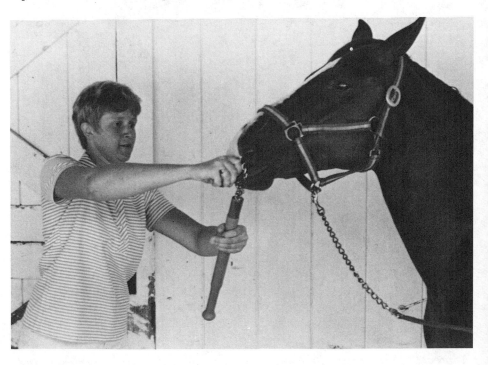

Still holding the upper lip, the handler twists the handle of the twitch to tighten the loop.

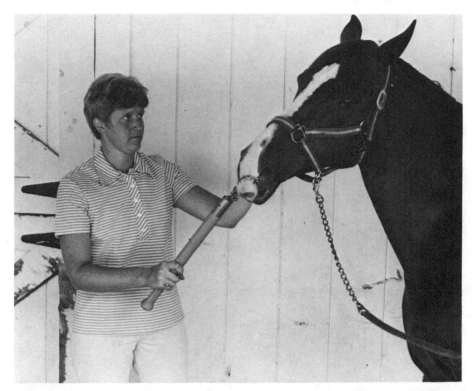

Twisted tightly around the horse's nose, the twitch causes discomfort without injury, making a very effective restraint. Most horses will stand quite still when held this way.

Some horses are so touchy that it is more than difficult to get a twitch attached to the upper lip. As a substitute, you can put the loop of the twitch through his mouth and tighten it around his lower jaw to obtain a restraint that is almost as effective.

When you are working alone and need to apply a twitch, you can make a "self-holding" twitch by adding a snap at the other end of the handle. Apply the twitch in the usual way and twist it tight, then snap the handle to the ring on either side of the halter.

In most tack shops you can buy an aluminum twitch device that uses a tightening screw instead of a loop of rope. Once secured on the horse's nose, it will stay in place by itself and you can snap a shank or your cross ties to the ring on the twitch to hold the horse where you want while you work on him.

In an emergency, a twitch can be improvised with a doubled

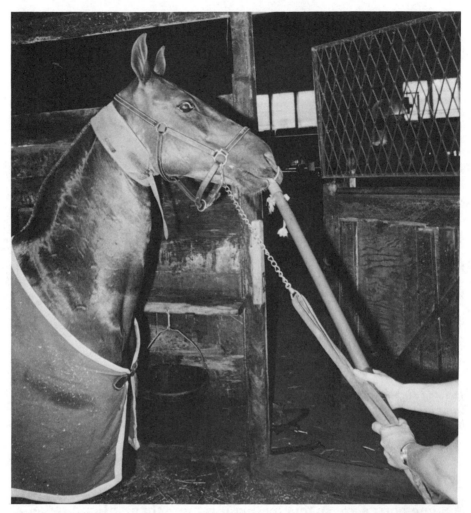

For a taller horse, or one that is quite fractious, a twitch with a longer handle is often very helpful, enabling a handler to control the animal from a greater distance.

loop of baling twine through any available handle such as the hanging hole in the handle of an aluminum sweat scraper.

Any kind of twitch, however, should never be used longer than actually needed. Ten or fifteen minutes at a time should be maximum. Keep it short, not only because you don't want to cause the horse unnecessary discomfort, but if you cut off the circulation long enough his nose will get numb, and when he stops feeling the twitch it will stop doing what you want it to do.

Another restraint device is a gag strap or gag rope—also known as a war bridle. They both work the same way. In its simplest form a gag strap consists of a four-foot length of one-inch webbing with a sturdy ring sewn in at one end. (A gag rope is a four-foot length of light rope, such as a sash cord, with either a metal ring or a nonslip bowline knot at one end.)

Place this strap over the horse's poll with the ring on the near side, an inch or two below the horse's ear. Bring the other end through the horse's mouth up his cheek and through the ring. It doesn't take much pulling on the loose end to hold the horse still.

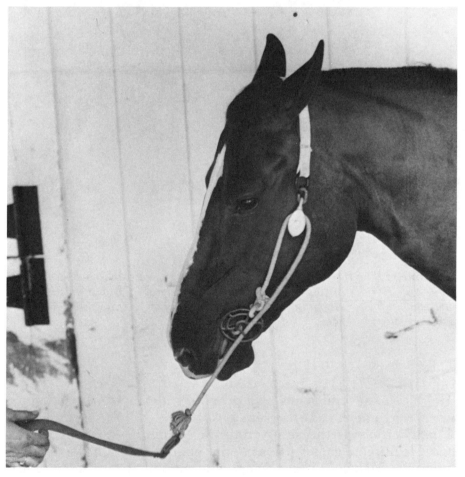

Another restraining device is the war bridle. This type uses a rope mouthpiece with cheek pieces and a pulley to achieve its effect. A simpler version can be improvised with a length of rope or strap fitted with a ring at one end.

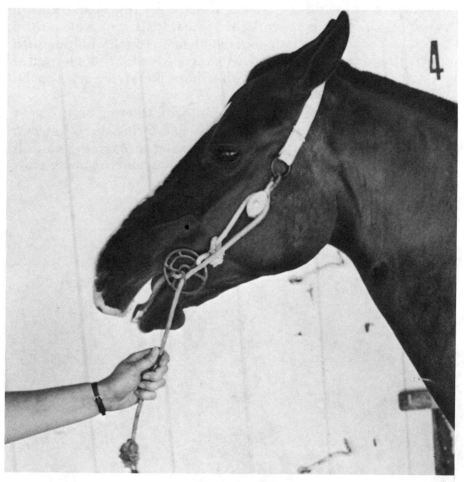

A moderate pull on the war bridle will apply enough pressure to restrain most horses. A war bridle arrangement is often used instead of a twitch. It is also sometimes useful for stopping horses that run away or to raise the head of a horse that starts to buck.

Hobbles of several kinds also provide a means of restricting a horse's movement and reactions.

Finally, there is the safety rope or "running W" which has several legitimate uses—when used properly. It can, however, be dangerous. Misused, it can cause serious injury to a horse and sometimes to the handler. It should only be used by professionals and experienced amateurs. The novice horseman who reaches the point where this device is the only thing that will solve his problem should send the horse to a trainer for a while rather than attempt the correction himself.

The general rule in applying restraints or punishments is: "Don't use a hammer to kill flies." If a "fly swatter" will do the job, don't subject the horse to something more severe. Use the mildest method that will get the result. Remember the purpose of the restraint is to prevent the horse from taking his usual escape route. This, along with reducing his fear and increasing his desire to obey you, provides the starting point for breaking many common bad habits.

8
Before You Begin

Everything we have examined so far suggests that horses' bad habits originate from one kind of bad experience or another. Usually, there is a combination of two elements: a stress situation that caused the horse to look for a way to escape from what he was asked to do, plus a handler who did not have the skill to alleviate that stress or prevent that escape.

Any effort to correct the problem carries the risk of making it worse. It is likely to revive the old stress. It will usually prompt another attempt to escape. And if the escape works again, it will further reinforce the bad habit.

For this reason, it is important to plan your efforts so that they will succeed, little by little. You want to be careful not to aggravate the condition. Doing that depends on thinking the problem through and developing a realistic idea of what is involved.

Before anything else, take a completely objective look at the situation and ask yourself some basic questions:

1. Is this behavior problem a habit that can be unlearned and replaced by desirable reactions?
2. Is this something that you are capable of dealing with? Is it within your range of experience and ability? A rider with limited experience should probably not try to deal with the more violent bad habits such as bucking, rearing, and running away. Leave them to a professional trainer or someone with more experience. In general, if you have even the slightest doubt about your own ability—even a little fear of the horse—you would be well advised not to attempt the cure by yourself.

For one thing, if you are afraid, the horse will sense it. He will hear it in your voice, feel it in your contact with him, see it in the way you move around him. If he knows you are afraid, he will certainly get no security feelings from you. Consequently, he won't be motivated to do what you ask. He is much more likely to take advantage of the situation to get his security in his own way.

3. Is the problem one that you are willing to deal with for as long as may be necessary to bring about correction? Would this horse, with the habit removed, be worth the effort required?

4. If you have decided you can and will do it, have you planned how, when, and where?

First, let's get a general idea of how to deal with the habit. For that you begin with a look at the probable cause for the bad habit. It is easy to overlook the simple, obvious explanation. Some years ago, a trainer told me about a problem he had had with a five-gaited saddle horse. In some classes he was a perfectly mannered mount for any amateur or child to ride. But other times he would buck violently. There seemed to be no reason for the misbehavior until the trainer realized that the horse bucked only when a certain saddle was used on him. Closer examination revealed that its underpadding was built up in a way that pinched the horse's backbone. By eliminating that discomfort, the trainer got rid of the problem permanently.

You should always look first for a physical cause of the trouble. Does the horse have any kind of injury or unsoundness you have not yet discovered? Is your tack and equipment suitable and does it fit properly? Does the habit disappear if you change equipment? Does the horse work better if you don't wear spurs—or if you do?

In short, don't look for hidden causes in the murky recesses of the horse's memory until you know there is nothing hurting him.

When you have eliminated physical causes, try to imagine how the habit got started. Examine everything you know about the horse's history that might offer clues to the origin of the problem. In particular, ask yourself whether your own handling may have contributed to, or even been the original cause of, the trouble. None of us likes to admit that we goofed. But if we do see ourselves as the source of the difficulty, at least we know more exactly what we are dealing with. At best, we have the chance to change the conditions and revise the methods. We don't, then, have someone else's errors to overcome.

The plan should include some idea of when you will work on the problem. In the general sense, "when" applies to a time relationship between your corrective measures and any other use or training of that horse. I have two general rules on that. I don't like to begin a course of corrective training unless I can continue it regularly until it gets results. And I don't believe in mixing habit breaking with other training activity.

If I know that my schedule of other activities is going to keep me from working with a problem horse at least several times a week, I prefer to leave that habit alone completely until I can give it the attention it takes to make progress. This applies more, or course, to the problems connected with performance than to stable vices dealt with in the daily routine.

I have found it unproductive to expect a horse to learn several things at once. If I have a horse that bucks, for instance, I would not school him over fences until I have the bucking under control. I might, however, leave the bucking alone and not ride him at all for a while, but break him to harness. I can teach him one thing—or another—but not both at the same time.

More specifically, your plan looks at the time in any given day when you can best make progress. For a horse that is nervous and easily upset, you should plan to work when there are few distractions or surrounding activities that would tend to aggravate the situation. With a horse that is barn sour, you would expect better results working at some time other than feeding time when you know he will be most eager to get back to his stall. And for almost any problem requiring slow, patient work, you should avoid times when you may be called away or forced to finish hastily before a deadline.

Similar consideration governs your selection of the right place for corrective training. One of the advantages you have in dealing with a difficult horse is that you can choose a location that gives you the advantage. Generally, an enclosed area is better than an open field or roadway. It puts boundaries around the horse and limits his alternatives. It also quickly becomes familiar to him, and that familiarity supplies a certain measure of security.

The choice is not always yours. The horse may call the shots and decide to rear or buck or balk when you had no intention of working on that habit. This is another reason why, with a horse of this kind—one with a habit that can show up occasionally—my solution is not to ride him at all until I am ready to begin a course of correction, nor to ride him anywhere except where the odds are in my favor.

Every time you ride a horse—for that matter, every time you go near him—you are either schooling or unschooling him to some extent. Every contact you have with him adds or subtracts a minute amount.

With an idea of what you will need to do—and when and where—you should also consider the equipment you may need. In some cases you will, perhaps, decide that a specialized item you don't have will be necessary. If so, it is best to acquire it ahead of time.

There are also a number of items that are useful in various situations. I have found a surprising number of uses for the following:

> Leather lead shank with chain and snap
> Lunge line with chain and snap
> Cotton rope shank or neck rope
> Bitting harness
> ⅝-inch rope, 50 feet or more
> Sash cord (emergency substitute: baling twine)
> "Hame" straps with buckles, various lengths
> Whips: lunge whip with lash and snapper
>   driving whip—five to seven feet long
>   riding whip or crop
> Blunt spurs
> Assorted bits
> Twitch

If someone would invent a device for controlling my temper, I would add that to my kit immediately. Getting mad at a horse when you are trying to break his bad habits will invariably produce negative results. There have been times—plenty of them—when a stubborn horse has worn out my patience. I've had to learn to recognize this and to keep an icy control on my emotions. When I feel that I can't do that—when my reactions start to get even a little out of hand, the best thing I can do is to stop immediately, get off the horse, and put him away until another day.

The retraining process requires complete objectivity. You can't provide that when your nerves are jangled. You may feel an angry determination to win your point if it takes all day. Trouble is, when you are in that state of mind it will probably take more than all day.

The reason is simple enough. Even if you have control of the impulse to beat the horse to a pulp, he will get the disquieting vibrations of your emotional state. It will create stress in him which, as we have discussed, is probably the cause of his problem.

The final point to include in your plan for dealing with a bad habit is to figure on getting help with certain procedures. For some things you may need expert or professional help. If it is

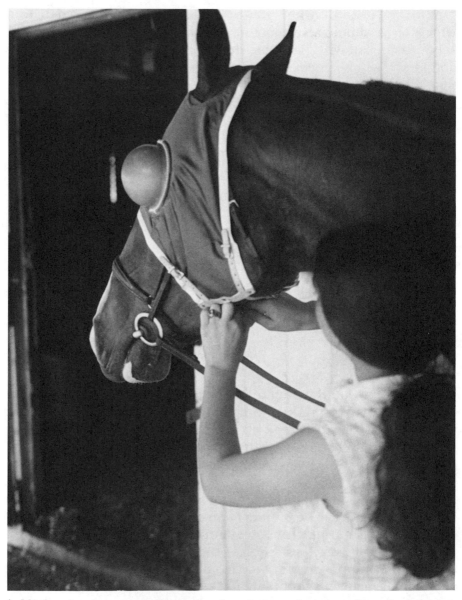

A blinker hood is a useful piece of equipment for a number of retraining activities. By blocking the horse's vision from sides and rear, the hood prevents the horse's being startled by the rider's movements. Blinkers also tend to concentrate the horse's attention on moving forward.

available, so much the better. But there are innumerable times when two people can accomplish a great many things that one person can't do alone.

For a number of problems under saddle, it is helpful to have an assistant holding a lunge line, ready to restrain if necessary, while the rider establishes communication with the horse.

Lots of times the helper is needed just to hold a piece of equipment or provide an extra pair of hands. He does not need to be experienced, but the assistant should be someone who is not afraid of horses. Naturally, if the same person helps you each time you work with a certain horse, the animal will get used to both of you and be less insecure than with strangers.

Careful preparation is an important part of making progress with your horse's bad habits. By thinking the problem through ahead of time, you can anticipate the scope of the job, decide whether you are able and willing to undertake it, determine how, when, and where to go about it. All these things are important because, as we noted at the start, an inept or ill-timed attempt at correcting a problem can make it worse instead of better.

9
Bad Habits in the Stable

There are horses ideally suited to your uses—horses that perform beautifully when you put them to work—that are something of a problem in the barn. Some of these difficulties may be a nuisance to you. Others may actually be harmful to the horse.

In general, these habits are expressions of nervousness or excess nervous energy. Confinement in a limited area is unnatural for horses. The vast majority of them adjust to the situation readily enough because their basic needs are cared for. So, for most horses, the four familiar walls are a place of security. So much so that frightened horses will usually try to get back to their stalls and will even run into a burning barn to do so.

On the other hand, some horses seem to have a stronger instinct for the natural, outdoor kind of life. In nature the horse keeps himself busy wandering and grazing, or just standing and resting when he wants to. Confined to a stall, he must eat when he is fed, drink when he is watered, and exercise when he is taken out. He often does not have sufficient natural outlet for his energy. This condition may lead to any of several bad habits.

Cribbing and Wind Sucking

In some horses, when the natural instinct to nibble and graze is frustrated by confinement, it is replaced by the substitute behavior of chewing on whatever is available.

Chewing on the wood of the stall leads some horses to develop the unpleasant and unhealthy habit of hooking the upper front teeth over a convenient post or ledge, such as the edge of a manger, and then arching the neck and pulling back to distend the muscles around the throttle, and sucking air into the stomach.

The habit is called "cribbing" and it falls into the category of habits that can be partially controlled but very rarely cured.

The terminology may vary. Some authors use "crib-biting" or "cribbing" to refer to horses who merely chew on wood. They use the term "wind sucking" for a horse that actually swallows air.

Whatever the term, cribbing is a serious habit and controlling it is important. A horse that cribs is hard to keep in prime condition. By filling his stomach with air, he tends to kill his appetite. He not only fails to get the nutrition he needs, but a cribber is more likely to be subject to attacks of colic which, of course, can be fatal.

Cribbing may not impair your horse's usefulness to you, but it will reduce his life expectancy, and it falls within the legal definition of unsoundness.

I am inclined to believe that there may be more than one reason why horses begin to crib. Some undoubtedly develop it in the course of nibbling on the wood. But it may also have its origin in insecurity.

I recently watched a ten-month-old colt playing in an enclosure where he could go up to the front of his mother's stall. Although he had been weaned for several months, he recognized her. And while he visited with her, I saw him grip the edge of the door in a motion that was much like an attempt to crib. Perhaps seeing his mother reminded him of his natural instinct to nurse. It seemed that actual cribbing might follow, if the situation created enough insecurity.

Whatever causes it, the question is what to do about a horse that cribs.

Coating the inside of the stall with a foul-tasting substance such as creosote is often suggested as a means of preventing wood chewing and cribbing. This may make you feel that you are doing something useful about the problem. But that is about all you will accomplish. Creosote won't stop a confirmed cribber.

The most usual way to manage the habit is to buckle a cribbing strap around the horse's throttle and keep it there whenever the horse is not being used. In order to swallow air, the horse must be able to expand the muscles around his gullet. A strap that is tight enough to prevent that expansion, but which does not interfere with breathing and eating, will keep him from cribbing.

The strap should be at least one or two inches wide. A discarded length of stirrup leather is often used quite successfully. It needs to be drawn quite tight. You can tell if it is adjusted properly by

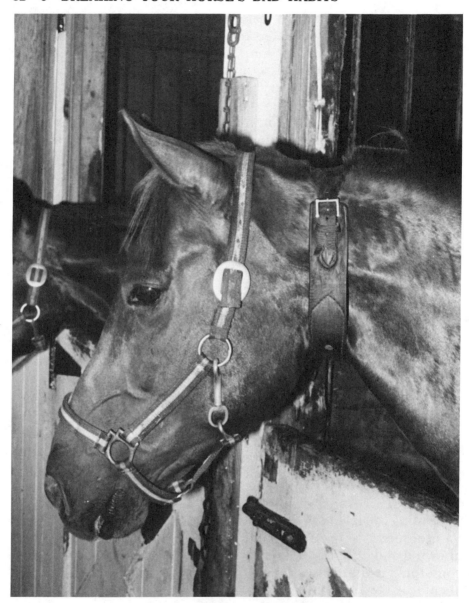

A two inch strap buckled around the horse's neck will prevent most cribbers from expanding the muscles around the gullet. This makes it impossible for them to swallow air but does not interfere with normal eating or breathing.

watching the horse. If he tries to crib but is unable to make the usual grunting sound signifying the intake of air, it is tight enough. If he appears to have difficulty swallowing, the strap may be too tight.

Tack shops sell a variety of more sophisticated improvements on the simple strap. They are designed to be less constricting when he doesn't crib and more effective when he tries to.

Many cribbers will still manage an occasional gulp of air in spite of the strap. For this reason, it is helpful to keep the horse in a stall that has no fixed protuberances or ledges on which he can hook his upper teeth and pull back. He should be fed in a removable tub rather than a fixed feed box or manger.

Note, however, that the horse must be able to arch his neck in order to distend the muscles around his gullet and swallow air. He can't do that if his chin is above the level of his chest. Eliminating all edges up to that height and raising his water bucket and feed tub will considerably reduce his chances of cribbing.

One very successful trainer tells me that he has cured some cribbers permanently by stringing electric fence wire around the

There are a variety of commercial cribbing straps. This one uses a shaped aluminum band around the gullet to provide more positive control and prevent expansion of the muscles in this area. Use of electric fencing where a horse may crib is also an effective deterrent.

inside of the stall along the edges where the horse hooks his teeth. After two or three shocks from the wire, the horse thinks twice about trying to take hold. It is a method that is worth trying. However, some cribbers are so inured to the habit that they will even put their teeth on their own knees or toes in order to swallow air.

There is also a way to prevent cribbing by surgery. An operation, sometimes performed in Europe, removes muscles around the gullet on the underside of the horse's neck. It has the disadvantage of making a noticeable change in the horse's appearance, and it has been rarely used in the United States. Most horsemen conclude that it is easier to control cribbing by other means.

Bed Eating

For much the same reason horses start cribbing, others become addicted to eating their bedding. A few acquire the particularly disgusting habit of eating their own manure.

Turning a bed-eater out to grass is, of course, an ideal solution. Where that is not practical, changing to another kind of bedding may be the answer. (Some stables give such a horse no bedding at all).

Where straw was once the almost universal bedding material, more and more stables are now, for economic reasons, using wood shavings, sawdust, peanut shells, ground corn cobs, dried sugar cane pulp, and other materials that horses are not likely to eat.

Besides changing to some unpalatable bedding material, you should make hay available to the horse more of the time.

You will see instances of a horse turning away from a rack of fine hay to eat straw from the floor. It does not happen often. But in some horses the grazing instinct is stronger than in others. For these horses, give up the hay rack and feed them their hay on the floor.

If a horse frequently seems to prefer straw to hay on the floor of the stall, you can suspect that the hay, which looks good to you, does not taste very good to the horse. Changing to another mixture may help considerably.

Unnatural appetites are also sometimes an indication of vitamin and mineral deficiencies and, in the opinion of some experts, may also be symptomatic of worms. If your horse persists in eating things you don't think he should, a checkup by the vet may be in order.

Weaving, Stall Walking, Stall Banging

It is hard to think of any explanation other than nervousness or boredom to suggest why a horse weaves, stall walks, or aimlessly kicks at the walls of his stall.

Weaving is a rhythmic, repetitive, ritualistic pattern. The horse stands in one spot and shifts his weight from one front foot to the other while swinging his head from side to side. A horse is rarely, if ever, observed weaving anywhere but at the door of his stall. This suggests that the habit may have its origin in the horse's attempt to find a way out of confinement.

Stall walking, similarly, is a nervous and repetitive pattern of endless walking around the stall or back and forth on a single path. This too, looks very much as if the horse is looking for a way out.

Stall banging is the annoying habit of intermittent kicking at stall walls or door with front or hind feet.

An exaggerated example of the weaving, stall-walking syndrome, this mare, owned by the author, will run back and forth incessantly if she is separated from other horses and placed in a paddock by herself.

What kind of nervousness brings on these habits? Some horses seem to have a stronger instinct than others for a free-roaming outdoor life. Some have more natural energy. Confinement makes these animals feel insecure, and they invent habits to relieve their insecurity.

There are things you can do that may help to discourage their responses to that insecurity. But the remedies will work best if you can relieve the pressure of the insecurity equation. Give your horse a more natural outlet for his energies. The more you can simulate your horse's natural condition, the more you'll tend to relieve his need for the habit.

Ideally, give such a horse more time in pasture or paddock. Let him satisfy his need for freedom and activity, and he'll have less energy to work off in the stall.

Giving him more exercise—riding, driving, lunging, etc—may also help. It's far from a cure-all, though. It consumes energy, but working under your control doesn't fully satisfy his need for spontaneous activity. A considerable number of Thoroughbreds in training at the race track develop these habits even though they are worked every day.

Some horses do less weaving or stall walking if they are given small rations of hay at more frequent intervals, preferably on the floor of the stall. It gives them a chance to simulate grazing.

Then, since a horse almost invariably weaves at the door of his stall, you might discourage him by completely closing the stall so he can't look out. Or, conversely, it has been observed that some weavers will stop if they are put in a stall with a window where they can watch passing traffic. Experimentation may bring you to a way of overcoming these habits.

Another suggested method is to hang two half bricks or blocks of wood in the opening over the stall door so that they divide the space approximately into thirds, vertically. If the horse starts to weave, he starts the blocks swinging on their strings and this distracts him so that he stops weaving.

In some cases it is not only confinement that brings on weaving. The habit may also grow out of the herd instinct and the horse's isolation from others of its kind. One of the best show horses I ever trained would weave when he was in a stable alone and stop when another horse was put in the stall next to him.

For this reason, some nervous horses who weave or stall walk—even some cribbers—will improve considerably if they have the company of a goat or pony in the stall with them.

Let's separate aimless stall banging—a nervous habit—from serious kicking, which is intended to harm a person or another horse. And we should also not confuse it with the eager clatter that arises in the stable when you approach at feeding time.

We are concerned with the horse that bangs intermittently with either front or hind feet for no apparent reason. The habit quickly ruins the walls or door of the stall, requiring frequent repairs. It may also result in injury to the horse's legs from the repeated concussions.

Again, turning the horse out, giving him more exercise, and feeding him small amounts of hay at frequent intervals often help to distract the horse.

To deal specifically with the habit, though, you should devise a mild but consistent chastisement that will reprimand the horse every time he does it. Several variations of a simple device can be used.

I recommend fitting a strap around each leg, just above the hock on a horse that kicks, or just above the knee on a horse that bangs with his front feet. From the strap you dangle an object that will rap him lightly on the cannon bone every time he kicks or bangs. The dangling object can be a few links of medium-weight chain. Equally effective is a block of hardwood about two inches in diameter hung on a piece of cord. Even a two- or three-inch rubber ball may do the job. The important thing is to rig it so that each infraction is immediately followed by a self-inflicted chastisement. It is the timing that is important, not the severity of the reprimand. Whatever you use to dangle from the strap, it should be suspended so that it reaches about halfway down the cannon bone below. Within a few days you should see distinct improvement in all but the most stubborn cases.

I knew an old horseman years ago who seemed to have a special knack with problem horses. "Old Red" had spent so much of his life with horses that he practically "spoke their language." A nervous young stud was sent to board with Red—a horse that fretted and banged in the stall a lot. With infinite patience, Red's response was one that few people have the time to try. Whenever the horse started to fret and bang, Red would snap a shank on his halter, lead the stud out and walk him for twenty minutes. Rain or shine, day or night, Red kept it up.

I saw the horse again a month or so later. He was a changed animal. He was quiet in the stall. He seemed calm and secure. Red's attention had overcome the horse's confinement insecurity.

Kicking

Horses that kick at people intentionally are another matter, altogether different from stall bangers. Much as we may hate to admit it, there are a few horses that are distinctly bad-tempered, vicious, and dangerous. Their habits should not be taken lightly.

As suggested in an earlier chapter, this kind of behavior may have started with the fears caused by defective sensory equipment. Strange as it seems, a blind horse is less likely to be mean than one with limited vision. Perhaps it is because a horse with a small eye can see enough to startle him while one with no vision has learned to rely on his other senses.

There are horses, too, who have become vicious as a result of cruel or inept handling by a previous owner. And there can be a very wide range in the amount of conditioning that makes horses resort to kicking as a defense. Some are relatively easy to cure; others are practically impossible.

The question each owner must answer is whether any horse that has a pronounced tendency to kick is worth the risks involved. For most novice horse owners, the only sound decision is to get rid of a kicker or get professional help in retraining a bad-tempered horse.

The plain and simple fact is that such horses can be very dangerous. They require skillful and experienced handling as well as love and patience. The novice may believe he has the necessary love and patience. But, while the horse may respond in time, he may just as easily fracture your skull before he finds out how loving and patient you *intend* to be.

In some respects, the horse who tries to hurt you every time you go near him is safer than the one with an erratic temper. The latter will lull you into forgetting to be careful. Then, when you are off guard, he may flail out and injure you.

If you have elected to try to redeem a kicker—and have accepted the risks that go with the decision—there are several basic techniques you should adopt. Remember, first and foremost, that kicking is an expression of fear. It comes from a balanced equation in which the confined horse has no way to escape and must defend himself against an approaching "danger."

One of the things that will unbalance this equation is gradually getting him to realize that your approach will not bring danger or discomfort so long as he behaves. Along with this he should learn to expect *consistent* chastisement if he does kick.

The first rule is to approach the horse calmly, quietly, slowly, and deliberately. Avoid surprising him. Speak to him as you approach his stall. Be sure he sees you coming. Give him a chance to anticipate you and recognize you as someone familiar.

The second and perhaps most obvious rule is not to approach him from behind.

Since you are trying to inspire his confidence and reduce his fear, it may seem like a contradiction to suggest that you begin by approaching him with a whip in your hand. But he has elected to pick up a weapon, so to speak, and you should be prepared to do the same. Teddy Roosevelt might well have been talking about dealing with a kicker when he advocated: "Walk softly, and carry a big stick." Your intention is never to provoke fear but to be ready to retaliate immediately when the horse makes the wrong move.

Obviously a horse cannot kick you when he is facing you, and he is most unlikely to do so as long as his head is turned so that he can see you with both eyes. It is only when his head is turned away that he can swing his quarters and kick you.

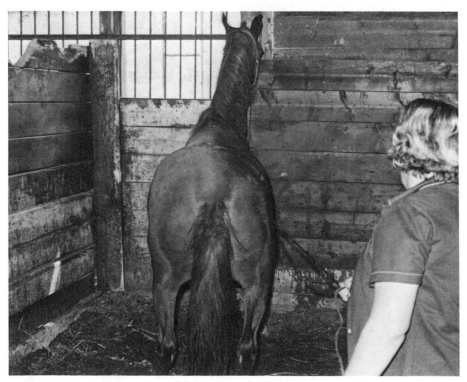

A horse that kicks should first be taught to turn and face you as you enter the stall.

Your first few lessons with a kicker will be to teach him to turn toward you when you come into his stall. Begin by teaching him to stand on the opposite side of the stall and watch you. Usually, you only need to show him the whip and perhaps rattle it on the side of the stall to direct him into the position you want him to take. If he tries to swing away and wheel into kicking position, he is entitled to one welt from the whip. And when you do it, don't be gentle about it. Let him know you mean business. The idea he needs to absorb is that he gets hit when he turns away from you. He does not get hit if he stands quietly or comes to you.

Once you are close to the horse, his kicking is less dangerous. If you are close to his hind legs, as you would be when grooming him, about all he can do by kicking is to give you a rough push. The kicking limb cannot travel far enough to develop a dangerous impact. It is when you are three to six feet away from him that he can do real damage.

Nevertheless, when I am grooming the hind legs of a horse that I know may kick, I hold his tail with the hand that is not busy with the brush. This accomplishes three things. First, it maintains a reassuring contact with the horse to reduce the liklihood that my movements will startle him. Then it provides me with a warning. If he starts to make a quick move, I can feel it coming. Finally, if he shifts his weight so he can kick, I can pull on the tail and bring his weight back onto the foot nearest me before he can raise it to kick.

In the long run, the things that reduce his fear and the consequent impulse to kick are the other things you do when you are near him. He learns from repeated daily contact that you bring him food, caress him by grooming, and mean him no harm. I prefer to give a kicker time to learn this before I try to teach him much of anything else.

For a considerable time after the horse seems to have lost his inclination to kick, you should continue to carry a whip and be ready to punish immediately if he reverts to his old habit. Each day that you handle him quietly and calmly will increase his sense of security and reduce the chances that he will revert to defensive behavior. But once a horse has gained a reputation as a kicker he should *always* be approached with a little more caution than other horses. "As long as he has feet," they say, "it's possible that he will kick."

Biting

Stallions are far more likely to bite than mares or geldings. This is partly related to a natural combativeness in the male. There are also mares and geldings that will reach out over a stall door to grab a passerby, and ones that will rush you with ears back and teeth bared when you enter the stall to feed them. Many will nip while you are grooming them or tightening the saddle girth. Regardless of sex, nervous and combative horses may resort to biting.

But the vice is more pronounced in stallions because it is related to their reproductive urges. In the courtship or "teasing" activity, nature has given the stallion an instinct to test the mare's readiness for breeding by nipping at her. Most colts with a pronounced tendency to nip will stop doing it as soon as they are castrated.

An interesting exception I once encountered was a colt who was orphaned at an early age. The trauma of losing his mother before a normal weaning time undoubtedly gave him a considerable sense of insecurity. The only substitute for his natural mother was being bottle fed by his owner. This made its mark on him. He was gelded as a three-year-old, but for the rest of his life he retained the habit of reaching for a human (as he had reached for the bottle) and nipping lightly whenever he felt nervous or excited.

Another example of nervous excitability was in a stallion whose behavior was usually exemplary. He would scarcely think of nipping at me unless a stranger came into the barn. But as soon as he heard an unfamiliar voice or sensed that someone he did not know was nearby, he would begin to nip. Obviously, nervous insecurity had something to do with it.

Properly handled at an early age, most colts learn not to bite. If you have one that has not yet learned, make it your business to punish him every time he tries it.

The easiest—but not the most desirable—thing to do is to smack him on the nose with the flat of your hand (or whatever else is handy) each time he reaches for you. It is perhaps better to smack him this way than to let him get away with nipping. But hitting him on the face will tend to make him head-shy, which causes other problems. It is much better, when you can do it, to crack him on the shoulder or rump when he tries to nip.

A sharply spoken rebuke also helps. The important thing is to condition him to expect something unpleasant when he nips at you.

While you are working on that conditioning and your stud is a little slow in catching on, there is nothing wrong with putting a muzzle on him while you groom him. It can save some wear and tear on you while he learns that nipping leads to something unpleasant.

For the horse that rushes you when you enter the stall with feed, a simple way to begin the conditioning is to throw a handful of grain in his face whenever he tries it.

If you have a horse whose habit is reaching out over a stall door to bite people or passing horses, a stall guard will prevent him from pursuing the habit. Another way to discourage the habit is to load a water pistol and give him a squirt of water in the face every time he tries.

Tearing Blankets

Some horses, out of nervousness and confinement frustration will, instead of cribbing or weaving, amuse themselves by tearing at their blankets. Other horses tear their blankets because of discomfort. If the horse's coat is not properly groomed and clean, a blanket may cause itching, and the irritation gives the horse a justifiable reason for wanting to be rid of it.

Similarly, if the horse is clean and the sheet is not, he may find it itchy and set out to remove it. But what about the horse who is thoroughly cleaned but goes after a brand-new or freshly laundered sheet? This is something you are likely to encounter if there is sizing in a new sheet, or if the soap used in laundering has not been completely rinsed out. A horse with sensitive skin may react violently to the effects of some laundry products.

But let's assume that you have made sure the horse is clean, and the blanket is clean or at least nonirritating. And let's assume that you have attended to the highly important detail of seeing that the blanket fits the horse properly. What then can you do about a horse that tears his clothing?

One thing you can do is leave blankets off him if he doesn't need them. Horses that are competing in shows probably need to wear sheets to keep their coats in show condition. But if it is not necessary and the horse hates blankets, letting him rough it through the winter is not a bad idea. Nature will take care of keeping him warm. He will grow as heavy a coat as he needs.

Another suggested solution is to coat the outside of the blanket in the area where your horse bites it (usually at the chest, shoulder, or flanks) with a strong-smelling yellow soap. If he really wants the blanket off, this probably won't stop him. But if he is

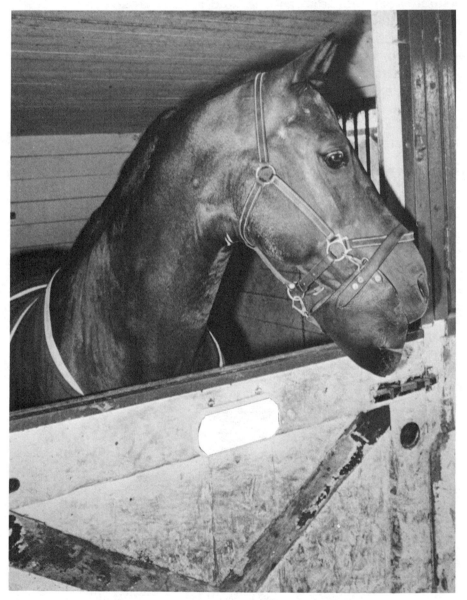

A leather bib will not prevent a horse from eating and drinking normally, but it will usually keep him from grabbing and tearing his blanket.

merely nipping at the sheet out of boredom, he may find the soap sufficiently distasteful so that he will take up some other "hobby."

Probably the most widely used method to stop blanket tearing is a leather bib. Fastened to the halter under the lower jaw, a bib will not prevent a horse from eating and drinking normally, but it will usually keep him from getting hold of his blanket.

If that does not do the job, a neck cradle or head pole may be necessary. Cradles are made in several types and designs. While they do not prevent the horse from raising and lowering his head and neck, they keep him from bending his neck to either side and from flexing enough to reach his blanket at any point. A head pole serves the same function. A cradle is buckled around the horse's neck and not fastened to anything else. A head pole of wood or light metal tubing is attached at one end to the horse's halter and at the other to a circingle, which also helps to keep his blankets from slipping.

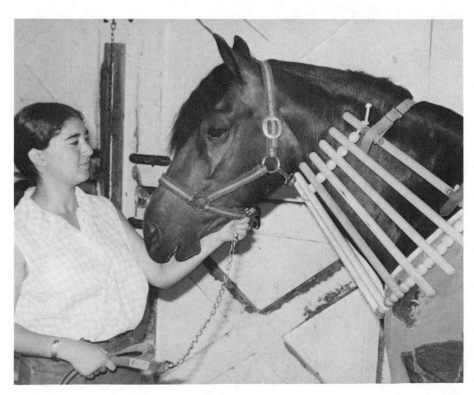

A neck cradle will prevent a horse from bending his neck into a position where he can bite and tear his blanket.

Mane and Tail Rubbing

Itching will cause some horses to rub their manes or tails on the sides of their stalls or—in pasture—on fence rails, trees, or prac-

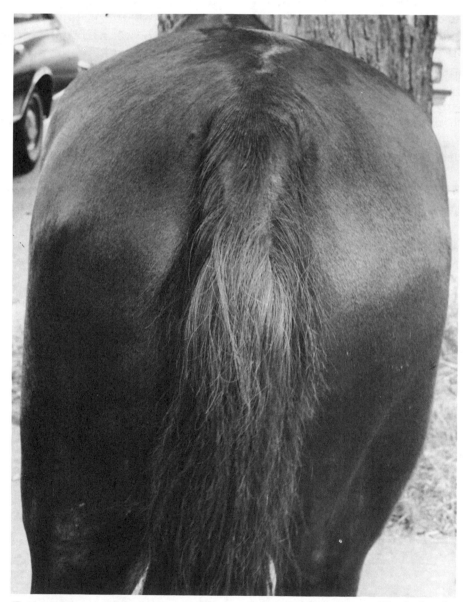

Tail rubbing quickly produces this characteristic appearance. The hairs that are broken off short seem to aggravate the itching condition that caused the horse to rub in the first place.

tically any other solid object that will serve the purpose.

Tail rubbing is often assumed to be an indication of worms. While this is a possibility that should not be overlooked, it is usually not the reason for rubbing.

Itching is occasionally caused by insect parasites such as mites, lice or ticks. Again, this is the rare case. Simple dirt or careless grooming is more often the reason for the itching that leads to rubbing. Then, when a horse begins to rub, he breaks off the long mane and tail hairs at the site. The result is not only unsightly but seems to increase the itching and desire to rub.

To correct the problem, begin by eliminating the cause. Carefully shampoo the affected area and then thoroughly rinse the hair until it is completely free of soap. When it has dried, rub the area vigorously with a good liniment to relieve the itching, stimulate circulation, and promote new hair growth.

After the initial treatment, continue to rub the area with the liniment each day when you groom the horse. Repeat the shampoo once or twice a week as indicated. Washing too frequently tends to remove natural oils from the skin and hair and may aggravate the itching. So be guided by the condition of the hair and skin and by the horse's apparent comfort.

Rubbing is a habit which may continue after the original cause (itching) is removed. You may need tail boards or electric fencing in the stall to stop some horses from doing it.

Tail boards, if you are not familiar with them, are usually made in the form of a horizontal shelf completely surrounding the inside of the stall at a height a little below the point of the horse's buttocks. They serve as a guard to prevent the horse from backing up and rubbing the upper part of his tail against the wall.

Electric fencing, obviously, will give the horse a mild shock if he tries to rub his mane or tail. Strung around the inside of the stall at tail level, it is a very effective deterrent and perhaps the most certain means of stopping mane and tail rubbing.

10
Correcting Problems of Handling

Most of the difficulties you encounter in handling horses are scarcely habit so much as lessons the horse never learned properly. It is chiefly the green colt that is hard to catch, hard to trim, or unwilling to stand tied.

Coltish uncertainties, however, do turn into established habits. Whether they are corrected early or late, their removal makes the horse more useful and enjoyable.

Hard to Catch

There are two reasons why a horse may be hard to catch in the stall or paddock. The first reason is suspicion because he doesn't know what you want of him—and the other is suspicion because he does!

Either way, he needs a reconditioning to expect rewards when he comes to you. A carrot? An apple? A lump of sugar? They are fine as far as they go. No harm in offering them each time the horse submits to your approach. But, as in the old legend that you can catch a bird by putting salt on its tail, first you have to get close enough to do it.

In one of his delightful books of cartoons, Norman Thelwell advises: "If your pony is hard to catch, take sugar lumps with you—and eat as many as you can, because you will need the energy."

There is a far more basic reward than sugar in terms of the horse's emotional needs. As we have emphasized before, his greatest psychic reward—far more important than his appetite for treats—is removal of fear and substitution of feelings of security. If the way you handle your horse *after* you catch him tends to increase his fear and reduce his security, there is no practical way to make him easier to catch. In this case the handler needs more training before he can hope to cure the horse's bad habit.

Obviously, a horse who learns that he will be fed if he comes when called, can also learn that he will then be ridden by someone with rough hands, if that's what happens. For this reason I suggest establishing certain priorities. If your horse is hard to catch, concentrate on simply removing that habit before you proceed with other training.

First things first. Let the horse become accustomed to you. Keep him for a while in a stall or small paddock where he will be close enough to see a lot of you and hear your voice frequently. Bring him his feed and water on a regular schedule. Speak to him. But ask nothing more of him for a few days. Take the time to be near him, speaking gently and moving quietly. Let him absorb the idea that your presence is not dangerous.

If he does venture to come close to you, let him. But make no move to catch him. Pat him if you can, or offer him a treat, but let him move away when he wants to.

As he becomes willing to approach, increase the amount of attention you give him. As soon as he will let you, begin grooming him gently while he is eating. Let him build an association between the pleasure of eating and the pleasant sensation of brushing.

Most hard-to-catch horses are head-shy. When you reach out to take hold of the halter, your hand sets off his optical alarm system, causing fear and retreat. To prevent this, a short piece of rope or strap, about two feet long, should be left hanging from the halter. It will enable you to begin taking hold of the horse gently without having to put your hand near his head.

Within a week or two, if this routine is followed with quiet assurance, the timid horse should be coming to you quite readily at feeding time and accepting your approach at other times. At this point you can begin introducing other light work which should also be planned so that each lesson rewards the horse with a feeling of security. More rigorous training should be delayed until all signs of being hard to catch are gone.

One very successful trainer makes it a point to reinforce the

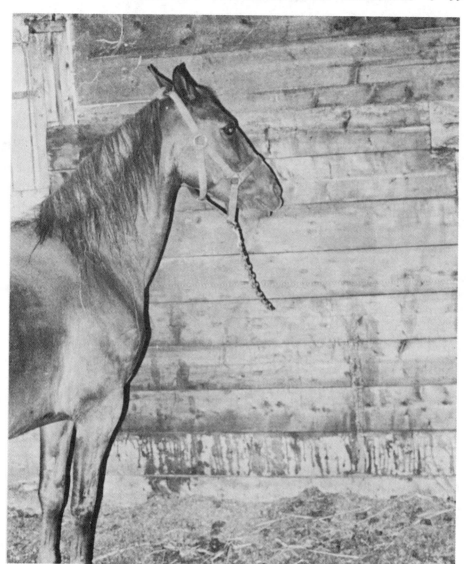

A short piece of lead shank can be left hanging from the halter of a horse that is hard to catch. It will enable you to begin taking hold of the horse gently without having to put your hand near his head in his line of vision.

conditioning regularly. When he finishes grooming or working his horses, he makes a practice of giving them a handful of grain *as he turns them loose*—leaving each horse with a fresh memory of reward to keep in mind when the time comes to catch him again.

Won't Tie

In a few horses, restraint alone is a source of fear. When these horses are confined, it takes very little to trigger a panic or escape reaction.

These are the horses which, with very little provocation, fly back when tied. The usual result is a broken halter and a loose (probably frightened) horse. It is another classic example of fear leading to an escape mechanism. With a little repetition it becomes a habit.

There are two schools of thought on the means of dealing with this problem. I have used both approaches successfully. It depends on the horse.

It is significant that 90 percent of the times that a tied horse tries to break loose, he moves backward to do it. If a horse's fear reaction directs him to move away from the thing he fears most, this preponderance of rearward escape movement tells us that he is most often afraid of something he perceives in front of him.

The one thing that is consistently visible in front of the horse in all these situations is the tie rope itself. From this clue we can deduce that whatever else it may be that startles the horse, it is his fear of the restraining rope that upsets some horses and causes panic. It becomes the dominant motivating influence.

A cure for the habit, then, depends on alleviating this dominant fear.

With a few young and skittish horses I have had good results when I allowed them time to learn that the tie rope itself does not lead to unpleasant consequences from which they cannot escape. The easiest way to begin teaching this is to snap a five- or six- foot tie rope on the horse's halter and simply let him wear it in his stall for a few days. Before long, of course, he will step on the rope, startle himself, and try to escape—from himself. Repeated a few times, this lesson usually teaches him that fighting the rope is no solution and the rope isn't really very frightening.

Meanwhile, I will be bringing him out of the stall each day for grooming, saddling, and other activities. With a green horse particularly, I use a pair of cross ties with enough slack in them to allow him to turn his head or move a step in any direction without immediately feeling restrained.

You can also use a piece of discarded inner tube as a shock absorber. Insert the rubber between the end of the tie rope and its fastening at the wall.

With a young and nervous horse, I often prefer to rig the tie ropes so they will come loose if the horse pulls hard on them. I would rather avoid a really frightening situation until he has a chance to learn that there is actually nothing to fear. Sometimes it is better to let him pull away a couple of times.

I proceed with the work quietly and reassuringly. If he makes no attempt to pull loose, that's fine. He gets an "A" for lesson number one. But if something does upset him so that he pulls sharply back, I let him go, taking the tie ropes with him. When he settles down, I calmly bring him back to position, refasten the ties, and continue where I left off.

This system can teach a young horse two things. First, he learns that there's no reason to be afraid of being tied. And he also learns that when he pulls away, the ropes he was afraid of go with him. After a few tries, a green horse usually learns that pulling away gets him nowhere, since he is promptly returned to the same spot.

But if he persists, he needs a more pointed lesson. If a horse habitually pulls loose and breaks halters—not because he is afraid of being tied, but to escape something else, it's time he learned there is a limit to what he can get away with.

For this you need a length of rope strong enough to withstand any strain he may put on it. And you need something to tie him to that will hold him firmly. A sturdy fence post may serve very well.

When you set this situation up, be very sure there is no way the horse can win the battle that is coming. If he does, you will make the habit twice as hard to deal with.

Some trainers secure the horse to a snubbing post with a neck rope. Instead of tying to the halter, they run the rope through the halter and fasten it securely around the horse's neck at the poll. This does provide a more secure restraint than tying by the halter. But it also carries a degree of unnecessary risk. A panicky horse can dislocate vertebrae in his neck and with a sudden forward surge he might even break his neck or choke himself to death.

A better method is to tie the rope around the horse's body. Make the loop around him snug but not tight. Secure the rope with a nonslip bowline knot. With the knot positioned under his body, pass the free end of the rope, then, between the horse's front legs, through the underside of the halter, and tie it securely to the snubbing post.

Once the horse is secured, give him time to discover that he can't get away. This is certainly not the time to punish him or provoke misbehavior. Don't go out of your way to scare him. But go about the routine activities against which he has previously rebelled. Don't force him to fight, but when it happens, step back

Tying the horse by a neck rope is one of the more common ways to discourage a horse from pulling back and breaking halters.

and let him learn his lesson. Pulling back will cause him discomfort; standing quietly will relieve it.

In a few really stubborn cases the lesson may have to be

The neck rope teaches the horse that the only way to release the pressure of the rope is to move forward, not backward.

repeated a few times. But most halter pullers catch on very quickly and give up their bad habit.

With any horse, there are times when there is work to be done that's likely to create problems. Perhaps the vet is coming to tube

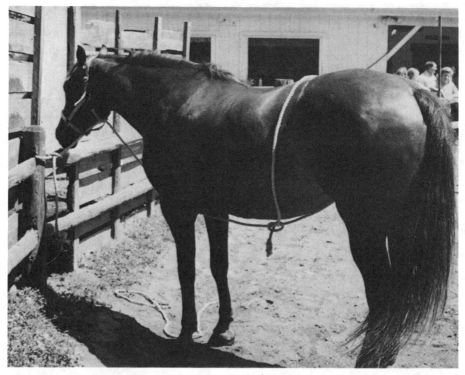

Many trainers prefer the use of a body rope instead of a neck rope to teach a halter-puller to stand tied.

the horse for worms, or you may have to trim the horse's ears for a show. For unfamiliar procedures like these it is generally best to untie him and hold him with a shank. Use a twitch if necessary, but don't force him to associate unpleasant procedures with being tied. It usually makes the trimming, or whatever, go better, too, since you won't compound his fear of the work you are doing with additional fear of restraint. The simple precaution may help prevent a bad habit before the horse learns it.

Hard to Groom and Trim

Only the wildest kind of horse presents any real problem in the course of routine grooming. If you can catch him and tie him, surely you can curry and brush him.

Indeed, it is the time devoted to the daily grooming that best helps build the bond of confidence between horse and handler. Through association with the pleasurable sensation of rubbing, scratching him where he itches, and the soothing strokes of brush or rag, your horse learns to equate your presence, your voice, and your scent with feelings of security.

Horses have their tender spots, though, where a gentler hand is needed. Eyes, ears, and nostrils should always be handled carefully. If you are not careful with a sensitive horse, he may develop an aversion to simple grooming.

A few horses are ticklish under the belly, back in the flank area. Others may be touchy around the hind legs. Common sense tells you to be careful, gentle and deliberate when you groom these areas.

At the same time, don't be totally silent as you work around your horse. A more or less constant flow of soft talking, whistling, or humming seems to reinforce his feeling of companionship and security.

Years ago, grooms were taught to keep up a constant hissing sound, not quite a whistle, made by blowing through nearly closed front teeth. It has a definite calming and settling influence on touchy horses. Perhaps it reminds them of the breathing sounds of others in a wild herd.

There are a few special procedures, however, involved in fitting and grooming your horse, especially for show purposes, where more special handling may be necessary to win the horse's cooperation. The most notable problem of this kind is the horse that is hard to trim.

Unless he has had a previous traumatic experience, your horse will probably learn quickly to accept the unfamiliar buzz of the clippers and let you trim his fetlocks, whiskers, eyebrows, and the small amount of mane you remove behind his ears for the bridle. Where you are more likely to have trouble is in cleaning the fuzz out of his ears.

This is one of the times when it is almost essential to have someone to help you. A horse that is hard to trim needs one handler to hold him and restrain him by twisting an ear or applying a twitch while the other handler does the clipping.

Make it your practice to trim as much as you can without applying the twitch. Let the horse learn that he won't be hurt as long as he stands quietly.

Don't approach from in front. Keep the clippers as much as possible out of his field of vision. With the clippers running in your hand, stroke his shoulder and neck so that he becomes used to the slight vibration and learns not to fear the sound.

With these precautions you can minimize the horse's reaction. But it is doubtful that you will ever completely overcome his resistance to having his ears trimmed. This is not a habit you are dealing with but a direct negative response to an unpleasant sensation.

Perhaps one horse in a hundred is quite different. There are just a few with a unique, violent and uncontrollable reflex triggered by trimming their whiskers. In thirty-five years of training and handling horses, I've encountered just three of them.

The first of these had been so badly mishandled by someone that he panicked if electric clippers were turned on anywhere near him.

The second was a three-gaited mare who presented no problems when I shaved her mane and tail. She was moderately touchy about her ears, but no more difficult to trim than a lot of other horses. But when I tried to take her whiskers off, it was, "Katie, bar the door!"

She and the third of this type, a Morgan stallion, reacted involuntarily, smashing and plunging in any direction. The use of a tranquilizing drug failed to control the reflex, and blindfolding only made it worse.

But there is a way, I discovered, to clean long whiskers off the muzzle of a horse that can't be clipped. Use an ordinary safety razor and gently stroke downward in the direction the hair grows. You will find you can shave off the long hairs without cutting the horse or nicking his fine coat. It may not trim quite as closely as clippers, but it is perhaps the only way with the rare horse that has this reflex.

If a horse suddenly rebels against clipping more strenuously than usual, check the condition of your clippers. A dull blade can cause them to pull instead of cutting. This hurts, and the horse naturally objects to that. Also, a short circuit in the clippers can give the horse a shock. If he doesn't react to that, there's something wrong with him. You can't improve the horse's behavior if you are using faulty equipment.

Hard to Bridle or Saddle

Few experienced horsemen ever have much trouble bridling, even with the horse that has a bad reputation in this respect.

The trouble most often occurs with beginners who don't know

the right way to put a bridle on a horse or with children who are not tall enough to cope with the task. It is hard to blame the mount for taking advantage of either of these situations. But the beginner can learn the right way and the child can get adult help or stand on a box to bridle his horse. Then if it is done the right way for a while, the habit of resisting bridling usually disappears.

What is the best way to bridle a horse? Let's take it a step at a time.

First, do it indoors. Outside, there are distractions that may cause him to shy and get away from you. Inside, you still have some control even if he should pull away.

Now, hang the bridle by the headstall over your left wrist. The brow band should be toward your elbow. Check the bridle to see that the straps are not twisted and the reins are not crossed.

Next, stand *beside* the horse's neck (on his left side, of course). Face the same way he is facing and place your left hand on his nose.

With your right hand, gently reach from behind, around his muzzle, to pick up the reins from your left wrist and pass them over the horse's head. Let the reins rest on his neck near the crest. By working from behind him this way you are out of his line of vision and less likely to startle him with your motions.

With the end of the reins around his neck, you can safely remove his halter. If he should try to move away, you could still hold him by gripping the reins together under his throat latch. If you are reasonable sure he *will* try to get away, it is wise to remove the halter and in the same motion rebuckle its headstall around his neck. This gives you a surer handle on him.

With the halter out of the way, repeat the motion of your right hand around his muzzle to pick up the headstall of the bridle from your left wrist. Notice that throughout this movement you are *not* standing in front of him where your movements could scare him, but you do have your arm around his head and your left hand on his nose so that you can hold him if necessary.

Now, raise the headstall with your right hand to a point just below the horse's ears, letting the bridle hang down over his face. Be very careful not to drag it roughly over his eyelids. At the same time, guide the bit (if there are two bits keep them together) toward his mouth with your left hand.

Here is where a surprising number of experienced horsemen have trouble. Pushing or banging a bit against a horse's lips or teeth won't make him *want* to open his mouth. He will throw his head up and try to get away. Squeezing the sides of his mouth with your fingers in only a little better. And there's a much easier way.

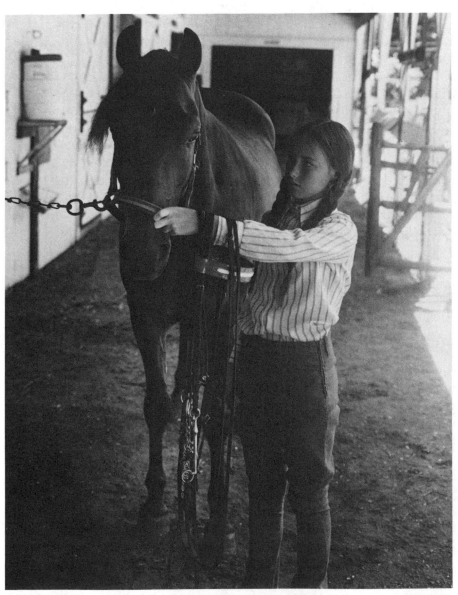

Bridling Step 1: Hang the bridle over your left wrist and, standing beside the horse's neck, place your left hand on his nose.

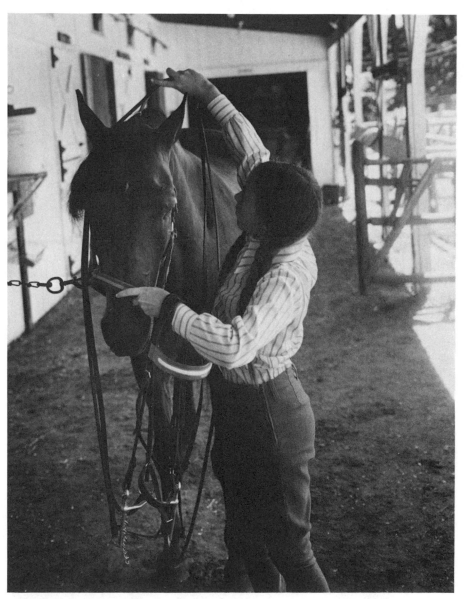

Bridling Step 2: With your right hand gently pick up the reins from your left wrist and pass them over the horses's head.

Bridling Step 3: With the end of the reins around his neck, you can safely remove his halter.

Bridling Step 4: Raise the headstall with your right hand and guide the bits toward his mouth with your left hand.

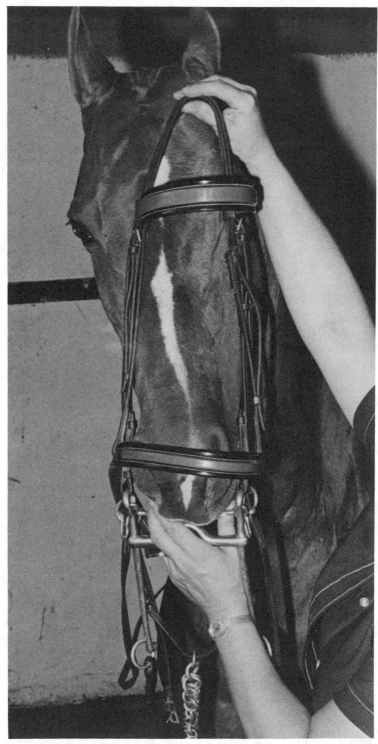

Detail shows how to hold the bits with your left hand to hold them together. To make the horse open his mouth, slip one finger into the corner of his mouth.

Bridling Step 5: Ease the headstall of the bridle over one ear at a time.

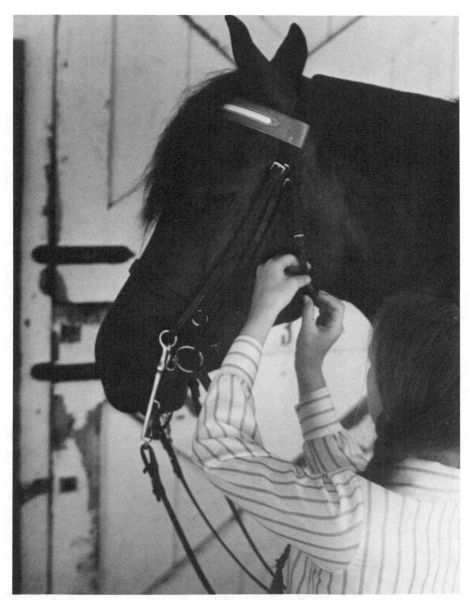

Finally fasten the buckles and curb chain, checking to make sure that all straps are straight and the bits are resting comfortably at the right position in the horse's mouth.

Most horses dislike the taste of a human hand. Slip a finger of your left hand into his mouth back near the corner where he has no teeth that could bite you. This simple trick will make almost any horse open his mouth. When he does, raise your right hand a little to pull the bit into position in his mouth.

Now, you've passed one big obstacle and there's just one more to get over. Some horses are very fussy about their ears and will fight any attempt to touch them. That is another reason for standing in the position described, with your arms around his head. He can't easily get away and you can easily get the headstall over his ears before he knows what has happened.

Whether he is fussy about his ears or not, however, put the bridle over one ear at a time. It is easier for you that way and causes less resistance in the horse.

Now that the bridle is on, all that is left to do is to fasten the throatlatch, noseband and curb chain. When you do, check the whole bridle to be sure it is straight and properly adjusted.

There is always the exception that proves the rule. There are some very head-shy horses that are hard to bridle even with this approach. Some will rear, strike, or bite. But the procedure described is still the best. In this position the horse can only nudge you if he tries to strike, and you can better control any efforts at biting.

If the horse raises his head too high for you, stand on a box or stool. You want to avoid rough handling of his ears or eyelids.

To cope with the horse that is extremely touchy around the ears, it may be necessary to unbuckle the headstall, get the bit in his mouth, and then rebuckle the headstall without pulling it over his ears. Usually, though, you will find after doing this a few times that you will gain the horse's confidence and from then on you will be able to bridle him in the normal way.

If a normally easy-to-bridle horse suddenly acts head-shy, look for a reason. An injury or sore place you had not noticed before might explain the trouble.

A word to the wise: Be equally careful when taking the bridle off not to hurt the horse's ears or eyelids. If he associates the bridle with pain, he will continue to be hard to bridle.

Putting a saddle on your horse's back is less likely to be a problem than bridling. If the horse does act frightened at your approach, move slowly and reassuringly. You may need to cross-tie him or have an assistant hold him for you. But if he is that timid about your approach, it may be best to spend a little more time winning his confidence before you try saddle work anyway.

Saddling Step 1: Lift the saddle high enough to clear the horse's back and set it gently in place. Be sure that the stirrups are run up so that they will not flop against a timid horse when you put the saddle on.

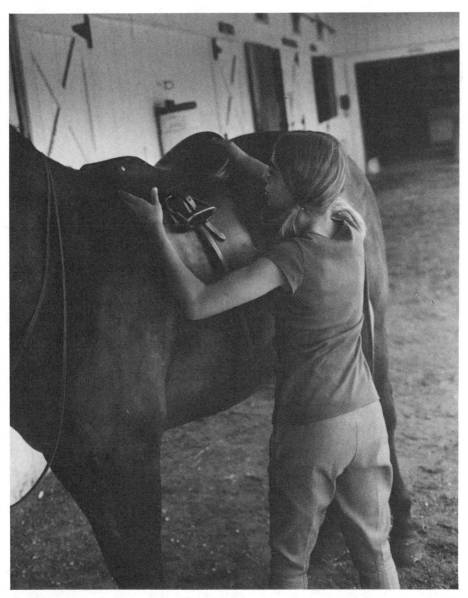

Saddling Step 2: Ease the saddle into the correct position making sure that the pommel clears the withers.

Saddling Step 3: Draw the girth up gradually, tightening one buckle, then another. A sudden pull can knock the wind out of a horse and even cause him to fall down.

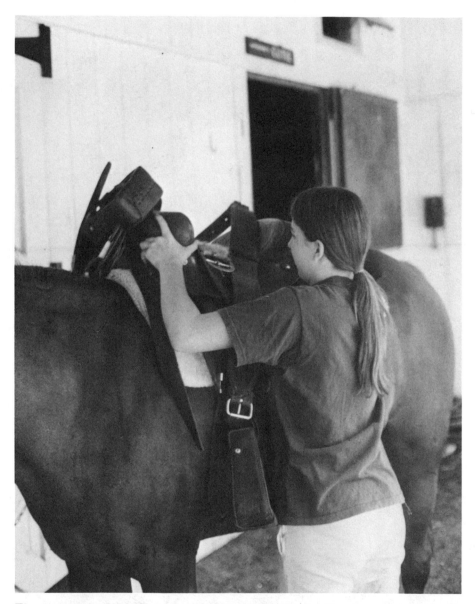

The western saddle, because of its size, is a little harder to put on gently. To prevent startling a timid horse, put your off stirrup on the saddle horn and lay the cinches over the seat of the saddle so they won't slap the horse's side as you set the saddle in place.

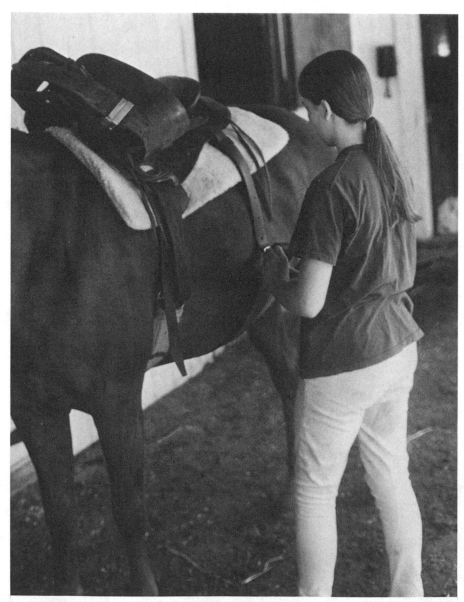

When using a double rigged western saddle (one with two cinches) leave the rear cinch loose to prevent discomfort that might cause the horse to resent the saddle or even make him buck.

Set the saddle in position gently. Don't let the girth or stirrups flop and bang him on the sides. A horse who has had a saddle thrown on roughly a few times learns to flinch from it. Undoing that kind of damage takes time.

All this assumes that the saddle you use fits the horse properly and does not pinch or chafe.

Now and then you may encounter a horse whose knees may buckle and who may even fall down when you tighten the girth. There are rare individuals who seem to suffer a physical "blackout" which is caused by sudden pressure of the girth. It is not a habit, of course, and it can be prevented by tightening the girth more gently. Set the girth loosely at first and then tighten it a little at a time until it is snug enough to hold the saddle.

Some horses have the annoying habit of reaching around to nip at you as you tighten the girth. This vice should be discouraged in the same way that you deal with other kinds of nipping. Make it your business to punish him every time he tries it. Give him a sharp word, a slap on the shoulder or a jab of your elbow. Along with the rebuke, be gentle in the way you tighten the girth so that he has less to object to.

Finally, there is the horse who has learned the habit of expanding his chest while you fasten the girth so that the saddle is loose when you are ready to mount. Handle this by setting the saddle and either waiting for him to relax or moving him a few steps and then retightening the girth before you mount. It is doubtful that horses "blow up" like this because they want to give you trouble later. They do it in anticipation of the discomfort of a tight girth, the way you might brace yourself if you thought something was going to hit you in the midsection. Take more time in tightening the girth. Doing it slowly will help overcome this habit.

Hard to Load

There is no more exasperating experience than when a horse refuses to load into a van or trailer. It is particularly annoying when you are in a hurry to get off early to a horse show or hunt meeting. But losing your temper or trying to hurry the horse along with force usually does more harm than good.

Most horses balk at loading because of some unpleasant experience in the past. They are afraid that the same thing will happen again. A particularly rough ride or a very long one might have made them anxious to avoid the discomfort the next time. It is not unusual for a veteran show horse to sulk at loading to go to a show but load eagerly for the ride home. He knows what is coming.

With a difficult loader, begin by making the surrounding conditions as favorable as possible. If the van is high and the ramp is steep, park where the ramp can rest on a little bank or hill so the horse can walk on more easily.

You often get good results if your trailer can be backed into a confined space or right up to the stable door so the horse has nowhere to go but into the trailer.

Padding or bedding on the loading ramp to deaden the noise is helpful, and the ramp should feel firm and secure when the horse steps on it. A rickety ramp may make him afraid of falling.

People are part of the conditions, too. Don't have too many around to confuse and scare the horse—three at most, and it is best if these are people familiar to the horse. Some horses are very touchy about strangers.

Your own confidence can be used to encourage the horse. Lead him up to the loading ramp *believing* that he will go right in this time. Don't look back at him. Don't give him time to think about refusing. Just calmly lead him as far as you can. It is surprising how many horses will respond and walk right in.

If he does balk, however, stay calm and keep him calm. After he has refused, let him stand quietly and think about it. He may change his mind and follow you after a minute or two, if nothing happens to upset him.

This is the point where many people try to coax the horse with sugar, carrots, or grain. These seldom do much good unless the horse is unusually hungry. He'd like to have the treat, but not enough to go into the trailer for it. The time for food is after he has gone into the van.

Throughout the loading, remain quiet but firm. Don't let him get away with murder. There's a vital principle, though, on the use of punishment. Let him know he is doing wrong—with a shout, a slap with the end of the lead shank, or a sharp yank at the halter—but *only if he moves away from the loading ramp*. Never punish him for standing quietly. There are better ways to get him moving forward.

One of the most commonly used means of persuading a horse to load is the "rope trick." A long piece of rope (three fourths of an inch or heavier) or a good web lunge line is drawn around the horse's hindquarters about midway between his hocks and the base of his tail. The ends of the rope are drawn forward along his

Loading Step 1: Lead the horse up the loading ramp confidently, believing *that he will go right in this time.*

sides to help prevent him from moving any direction but straight forward. Then a strong pull on the rope and some enthusiastic clucking are used to encourage the horse to move forward.

Loading Step 2: Don't look back at the horse or give him any indication of indecision that may encourage him to think about refusing.

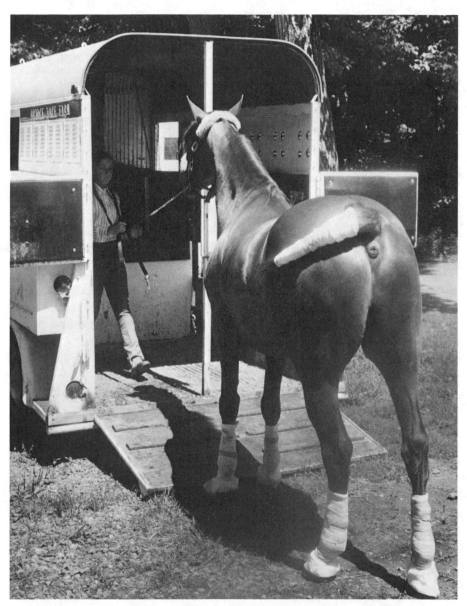

Loading Step 3: If he does balk, stay calm, and keep him calm. After he has refused, let him stand quietly and think about it. He may follow you after a minute or two if nothing happens to upset him.

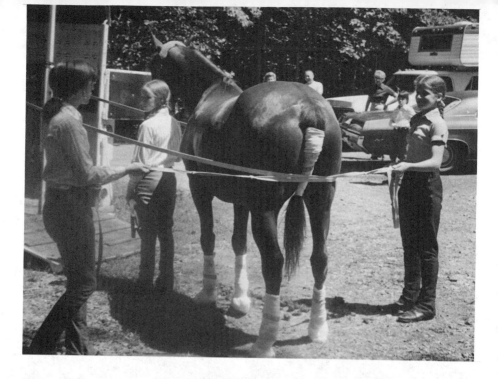

Loading Step 4: Two assistants with ropes or lunge lines drawn around the horse's hind quarters prepare to help load a horse that won't walk in by himself.

Loading Step 5: A pull on the ropes and some enthusiastic clucking are used to encourage the horse to move forward. The same result can be obtained with a single assistant and one rope fastened to the opposite side of the trailer.

When no rope is available, two people can accomplish much the same result by standing on opposite sides of the horse, locking hands behind him, and pulling him forward.

This works well on many horses. After a few experiences with it, many a formerly hard-to-load horse will walk right into the van at the first sight of the rope. However, there is little sense in persisting with the method with any horse—and there are plenty of them—that will fight the rope.

For these, this is a better way: Lead the horse as close as possible to the ramp. Usually he will stop just inches short. Then, while one person holds his head straight and gently coaxes him toward the van, two assistants on either side of the horse move his feet up one at a time. First one front foot is picked up and placed on the ramp, then the other. Don't try for too big a step at a time.

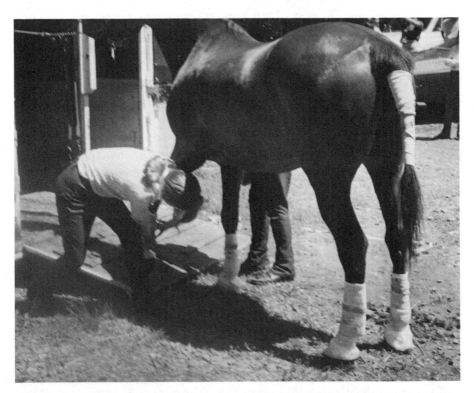

Loading Step 6: For a horse that fights the rope, the assistants can help by picking up the horse's feet one at a time and placing them on the loading ramp. Once they get their feet on the ramp, many horses will decide the trailer is safe and will walk in the rest of the way.

With the front feet firmly on the ramp, the hind feet can be moved up one at a time. The whole process may have to be repeated two or three times while the horse tries your patience by immediately retracting the foot you have just moved up. But stick with it. Even if the horse backs all the way off the ramp a time or two, just calmly work him forward again. Before long the horse will probably make up his mind that it is safe and walk quietly in.

Patience is the essence of this technique. It may take a little more time, but in my experience it has worked where all else has failed because it gives a horse confidence instead of insecurity.

If you expect to transport your horse frequently, it may be worthwhile to investigate different types of conveyances. A tall, high-headed horse, for instance, is more likely to load into a vehicle with more head room. A surprising number that won't walk up a tailgate loading ramp will get right into a step-up type of trailer. Others do just the opposite. The right equipment for hauling may save many hours of annoyance over loading.

A word about hauling your hard-to-load horse with other horses: There is no rule about which one to load first. The hard loader may like the company of other horses and may load more willingly if another horse is already in the van. On the other hand, he may find it more inviting if he is not being crowded into cramped quarters. Experiment both ways to see which works best.

Some useful tricks for loading horses are discovered by experimentation or by accident. I had one horse that fought and kicked if anyone got close behind him to help me load him. The solution, it turned out, was for my assistant to stand ten yards behind the horse and toss a pebble or two at his rump. It worked every time.

Another recalcitrant loader needed only the sound of someone scratching the ground behind him with a metal lawn rake to make him prefer the safety and comfort of the trailer.

If your problem horse is one you intend to keep and may load again sometime, avoid the brute force methods. The horse will only get progressively worse. While horses can be dragged into a truck with a winch, or blindfolded and led up the ramp (which is not always successful) such methods only make matters worse. What pays off in the long run is taking the time to teach your horse that the van is nothing to be afraid of. When you do that, you solve the problem permanently, not just for this trip.

Some horses load readily enough, but travel badly. A sudden panic may seize them and cause them to thrash, lunge, leap or fall down. Some seem to fear the confinement of the unfamiliar enclosed vehicle. A friend of mine owned a mare that would only travel lying down.

It sometimes helps to load the horse at home, feed him in the van and unload him without going anywhere. Do this a number of times so that the horse will have a chance to associate the van with comfort, food, and security. It may help when it comes time to travel with him.

But not always. I had one horse who had been traveling to horse shows by trailer from the time he was weaned until he was four. Then, quite suddenly, a minor mishap scared him. He got the heel of his right hind shoe caught under the partition in the trailer. Unable to move his foot naturally to adjust his stance and balance with the movement of the trailer, he started to struggle and eventually ripped the shoe off.

From that day on, he had a conditioned fear. If his right hind foot touched the partition, he would begin to scramble violently, throwing himself against the opposite wall of the trailer. But if he could ride with the partition pushed away from him on the right, so that his hind foot didn't touch it, he was gentle as a lamb. It only took about four inches of extra space to satisfy him. But that extra four inches made all the difference in the world.

I have known horses that would ride in a trailer but not in a truck; others that were fine in a truck and would have no part of a trailer. And there was one who would only condescend to travel if the conveyance—truck or trailer—was open on top. I've known many who would ride better facing backward, a few who preferred to face front.

It would take a considerable fleet of diverse vehicles to have the right one to suit every finicky horse. For one that travels badly it is now quite usual to administer a tranquilizer before each trip. You may not need to continue this. After five or six trips under the influence of the medication, some horses will turn into placid passengers.

For the few that never do lose their fear of transportation—after you have exhausted all other reasonable possiblities—the only solution may be to tranquilize the horse every time you need to move him, or else leave him at home.

Before tranquilizers were available, I was campaigning a horse that had some reason to hate trailers. Before I got him he had been in transit one winter night when the trailer skidded into a ditch. He spent a number of miserable hours, cold and wet, trapped in a trailer lying half on its side. He was good enough at shows to be worth the trouble, so I put up with difficulties in loading him for a couple of seasons. Eventually I gave him away to a good home where I knew he would never have to travel again.

Trouble was, the man I gave him to died before the horse did and I got the horse back. When I found another home for him, I prepared for the usual struggle to load him one last time to get there. With the perversity typical of horses, to take the last trip he ever made, he walked right into the trailer without the slightest hesitation!

Hard to Shoe

Your farrier undoubtedly knows more ways to handle a recalcitrant horse than we could hope to cover in a book of this kind. Most of us find, however, that a busy horseshoer can ill afford to waste time on an uncooperative horse. Such a horse is not only dangerous, but in the time it takes to shoe him, the man could make three times as much money with horses that behave. So if you can get the blackskmith to come and work on your troublemaker, you'll rarely find that he has time to be patient.

It's to your advantage, then, to do all you can to prepare the horse for the farrier's visit.

A horse that is handled and groomed regularly soon gets used to allowing his feet to be lifted one by one as you pick dirt from his hoofs. To avoiding scaring the horse, the experienced handler speaks softly, strokes the horse on the shoulder, then gently runs his hand down the leg to the fetlock. By squeezing here with your hand and leaning your shoulder against the horse to shift his weight off the foot you are trying to lift, you can raise the hoof from the ground with no trouble.

Once a horse becomes comfortable with the idea of having his feet lifted and held, the only part of the shoeing process that is likely to bother him is the hammering necessary to drive and clinch the nails. Here again the problem is usually fear of the unfamiliar, since the process is not painful (unless the horse has suffered an injury or is lame in that foot). By making it a regular practice to tap the foot, lightly at first, then more vigorously, with your hoof pick or even a small hammer, you can turn an unfamiliar experience into an accepted part of the horse's routine.

If the horse exhibits unusual distress when you work on one foot but not the others, something may be hurting him. You may need a consultation with your vet to correct the physical problem before you can hope to win cooperation.

A horse that is handled and groomed regularly soon gets used to allowing his feet to be lifted one by one as you pick dirt from his hoofs.

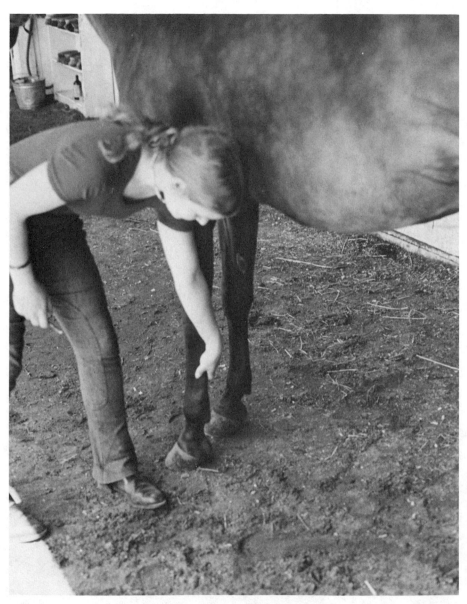

It is easier to pick up a horse's foot if you lean against his shoulder with your shoulder to shift his weight off that foot.

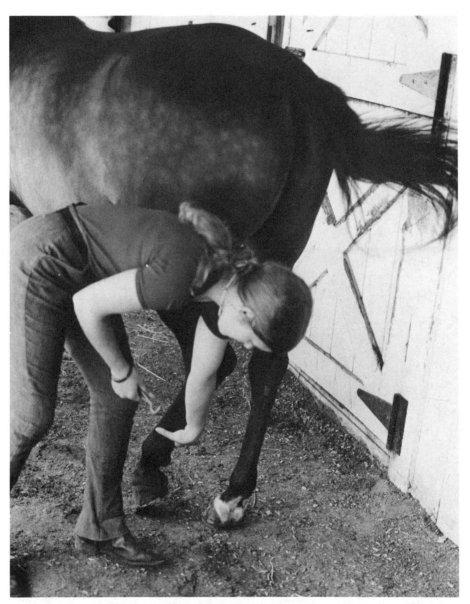

The technique is similar with the back feet. Gently run your hand down the leg to the fetlock, squeeze here with your hand and lean your shoulder against the horse to shift his weight off the foot you are trying to lift.

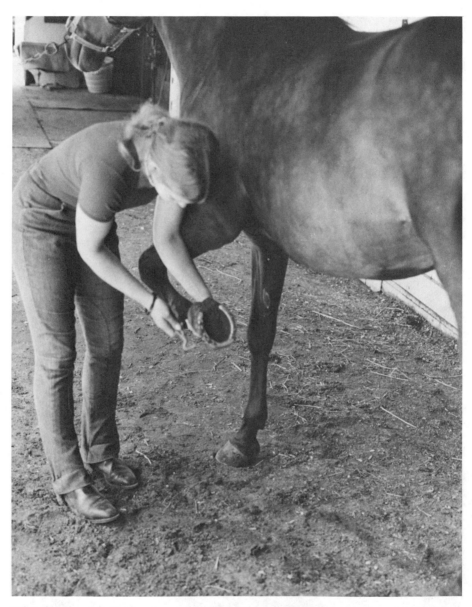

The only part of the shoeing process that is likely to bother a horse who has been handled regularly is the hammering. You can prepare for the farrier's visit by tapping the hoof until it becomes an accepted part of the daily routine.

Another trick worth trying on a horse that is consistently touchy around his feet is to put blinkers on him so he can't see what you are doing. It is a technique that works with some, and may make others worse.

Some horses will take advantage of your gentle approach and exhaust your patience. Losing your temper and punishing a horse that won't let you hold his foot up won't improve him. One device that may work is called a Rarey strap (named for the trainer who invented it). It is a wide strap, thirty-six to forty inches long, with a buckle at one end. Next to the buckle on each side of the strap are loops or keepers. The strap is first looped snugly around the pastern with the end through one keeper. The foot is then lifted and the end of the strap passed around the forearm or gaskin and buckled up tightly. Applied properly, the strap will prevent the horse from putting his foot down until you release him. Expect the horse to struggle quite a bit when he finds himself restrained this way. He should be kept in his box stall or other enclosure where he can't hurt himself. Given some time to thrash around and fight it out by himself, he will find that he can't get that foot down and will finally accept it and stand. Then you can approach him, rag him all over gently, talk to him reassuringly, and release the strap.

As one of the more extreme methods of imposing your will on the horse, the Rarey strap should not be adopted as a substitute for patient training. It is better to accustom the horse to a new procedure and gain his confidence. Use of the Rarey strap is a last resort for a stubborn or spoiled animal. I strongly caution against trying this with makeshift equipment or a strap that is not strong enough to withstand the horse's struggles. If he learns he can get free by fighting hard enough, you will have more trouble than you started with.

11
No Mouth, No Horse

There's an old saying: "No mouth, no horse." And it is hard to dispute the concept that the quality of the mouth has a very distinct bearing on the usefulness, performance, and enjoyment you can get from your horse.

There's not much physical difference in the oral cavity of the horse with a good mouth and one with a bad mouth. The lips, tongue, teeth, bars, and other parts that make up the mouth area are much the same in all horses. What differs is the sensitivity and acceptance of the bit. The horse's response to commands through the reins may vary greatly, and many behavior problems under saddle originate in mouth problems.

Proper development of the horse's responsiveness to the bits is unquestionably the most important part of his training. If the rider cannot communicate his wishes to the horse through reins and bits, he loses the most important means of telling the horse what to do. Lack of communication sets up stress situations, and stress leads to bad habits.

Getting the mouth right may not automatically cure an established bad habit. But failing to do so will probably keep you from making any progress in breaking it.

A bridle and bit (or hackamore) are intended to bring pressure at a point where the horse is sensitive. With a minimum amount of strength, the rider should be able to control and direct the far superior strength of the horse. The bridle is designed to bring pressure, though, not pain. If it *hurts*, the horse will soon begin to look for ways to escape from the pain. The habits that develop as a result may take many forms: head tossing, star-gazing, boring, sidling, propping, rearing, kicking, bucking, and impatience to

A horse that fights the bit with stiff neck, open mouth and raised, extended nose, will usually need mouthing before any other bad habits can be improved.

break from a walk to a trot or from a trot to a canter. While the horse that runs away is commonly assumed to have a bad mouth, it is less often understood that the balker may have also acquired his habit in the same way.

A few horses do have a physiological problem in the mouth. You should check carefully for this before you plan any strategy for breaking the bad habit. A severe parrot mouth or undershot jaw, for instance, is an abnormality that could cause trouble. If the teeth do not meet normally, the horse's first molars (top or bottom) will grow abnormally long, and some horses learn to take the bit against these insensitive molars and go their merry way. The old saying refers to "taking the bit between the teeth." This probably never actually happened. But the horse that can take the bit *against* his back teeth can assume control of the rider.

Other problems with the teeth are a more frequent cause of trouble. In normal use, most horses' back teeth tend to wear

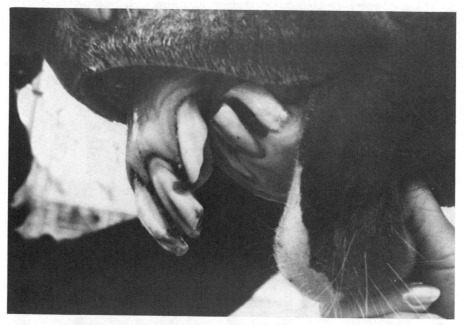

Physical problems such as "parrot mouth" are rare, but they can cause serious difficulties in developing proper responsiveness to the bridle.

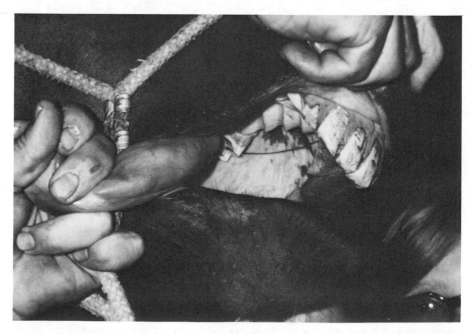

When the teeth do not meet properly, the first molars grow abnormally long as shown here. These molars may cause pain, or the horse may learn to take the pressure of the bit against the insensitive teeth.

An undershot jaw, the opposite of "parrot mouth," is equally troublesome.

somewhat unevenly so that they develop sharp points or hooks at their outer edges. As these grow more pronounced they may impair the horse's ability to chew his food. And the sharp protuberances are likely to cause him considerable pain when he wears a bridle. The cheek pieces, noseband or cavesson will squeeze his cheeks against the sharp corners on his back teeth. This hurts, and he resorts to some escape from the pain. He no longer carries his head in the desired position. He may become balky or fretful. He may even give the appearance of being lame. He begins to show one kind of unwanted behavior or another.

The habits he acquires as a result, although they vary widely on the surface, all trace to the discomfort he feels in his mouth.

There are also several diseases of the mouth that can cause problems, at least temporarily. If the horse is asked to work in the normal way while suffering one of these conditions, the bit will hurt. If the cause is not discovered and the work is continued, the horse may seek an escape and establish a habit that remains after the inflammation is gone. It is easy, then, for a subsequent owner to blame the horse's basic disposition. Why not? You have no other way of knowing or detecting the original cause.

Among the disease problems that may bring sudden disobedience to the bridle are stomatitis, lampas, and glossitis—three types of inflamations that cause pain and swelling in the mouth. There are horses, too, with excessive or inadequate secretions of saliva. In general, the horse that salivates excessively does it more from nervousness than from any organic cause. The copious flow of saliva is not a problem in itself. But it may be a clue that the horse is fretting too much and that he might benefit from retraining and rebitting.

Inadequate salivation—"dry mouth"—on the other hand, is usually organic in origin and will often interfere with the horse's responsiveness.

Some horsemen are sucessful in getting the saliva flowing more normally by giving a dry-mouthed horse sugar or salt after bridling him. Another method is to fasten a small cloth bag filled with potassium chlorate to the bit so it will rest in the horse's mouth on his tongue.

Finally, there are horses whose mouths have been damaged by abuse or accident. Repeated abuse with severe bits and heavy hands can damage the tissues where the bit normally rests and impair or destroy their sensitivity. It is a problem all too commonly found in polo ponies.

I recall, also, a very promising young stallion whose jaw was broken in a training accident. From then on, no attempt at training by the best professional available was ever completely successful. Despite many changes of bits and great patience, the horse was never able to wear a bridle and carry his head correctly flexed. Attempts at forcing him to accept the bit brought violent temper tantrums, even though he was otherwise cooperative and easy to handle. The injury, obviously, left him with a condition that caused pain.

The first step in curing any of the bad habits that stem from the mouth is to eliminate the cause. If pain was the stimulus that originally conditioned the response, you won't have much luck in reconditioning until you remove the pain.

How? Begin by examining the horse for signs of soreness in and around the mouth. Look inside as well as outside. If you are not sure, call in the vet.

You won't need any help to discover the cuts or sores at the corners of the mouth, caused by an ill-fitting bridle, which naturally causes negative, if temporary, reactions.

But trouble with the teeth may not be so easy to spot. If an examination reveals sharp points, they should be "floated" or filed down. A horse that has had trouble of this kind will probably develop it again as his teeth wear more. Any mature horse should have his teeth checked at least once a year. Some will need floating more often.

Besides hooks on the back teeth, a surprising number have "wolf teeth" which may cause trouble. Wolf teeth are vestiges of an additional pair of pre-molars that horses had in an earlier stage of evolution. They usually appear in the upper jaw but may also be found in the lower. Some horsemen prefer to leave them alone so long as they cause no problem. But these wolf teeth often grow long enough—and typically crooked enough—to cause discomfort and poor response to the bridle. If so, consult the vet about removing them.

Beyond checking the mouth itself, be sure that the bridle fits properly and that the bit or bits are in the right place in the mouth.

The selection of the right bit is an art in itself. There are almost limitless variations in sizes, styles, designs and types of bits. The differences between them are often subtle. But by slight changes in the amount and location of the pressure they apply, the resulting effect may be vastly different.

Bits are of two kinds. There are direct-action bits, commonly called "snaffles." By pulling on either or both reins, the rider brings pressure on either or both sides of the horse's mouth—the amount of pressure being the same as the amount of pull exerted. The other type is a lever-action or curb bit. The amount of pull is increased by the mechanical advantage of the lever. There are also hackamores that apply pressure outside the mouth, and there are combinations of the basic types.

Generally, direct-action bits are more useful for raising a horse's head. They also give a more distinctive signal for steering, since pressure can be applied to either side of the mouth selectively. The lever-action bit usually applies some pressure on both sides of the mouth even when only one rein is tightened. The lever-action bit also tends to increase flexion at the poll more than the direct-action bit.

The severity of any bit is affected by the diameter and surface of the mouthpiece. The thicker bit distributes the pull over a wider area and is therefore milder than a bit with a sharp mouthpiece. Generally, the heavier the bit, the gentler its action. In any lever-type bit, the length of the shank is the most important gauge of severity. A longer lever increases the mechanical advantage so that a slight touch on a long shank curb may produce far more pressure than pulling with all your strength on an egg-butt snaffle.

Whether you need a bit that is less severe or one that gives you

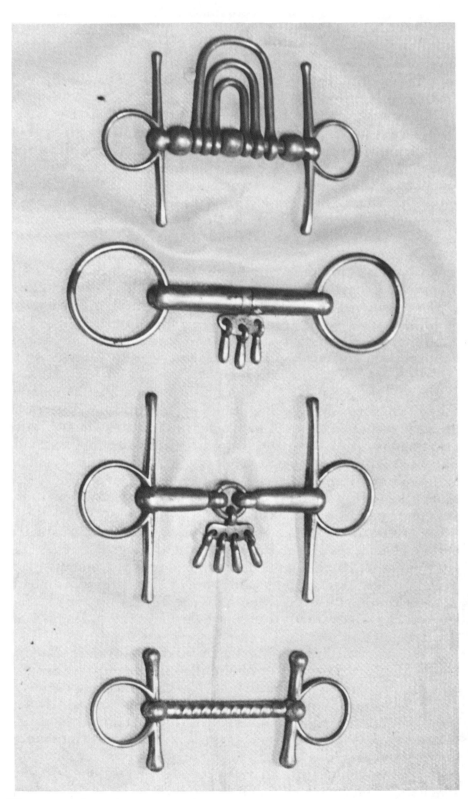

There is an almost limitless number of variations in the sizes, styles, designs and types of bits. Shown above are four distinct types used for mouthing colts.

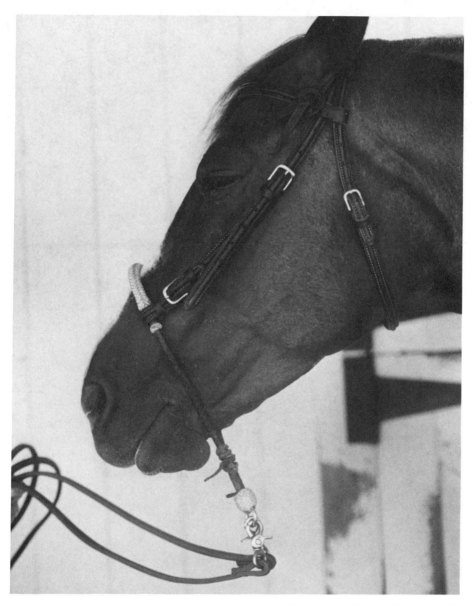

The bosal-type hackamore applies pressure outside the horse's mouth to provide the rider control over his movements and gaits.

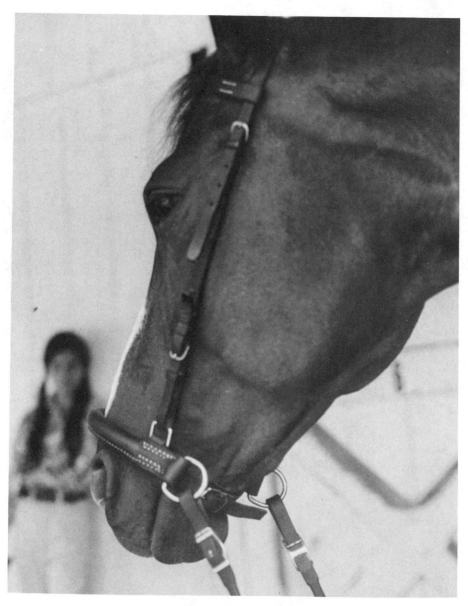

Another type of hackamore that may be useful for retraining a horse who has learned to resent and resist conventional bits.

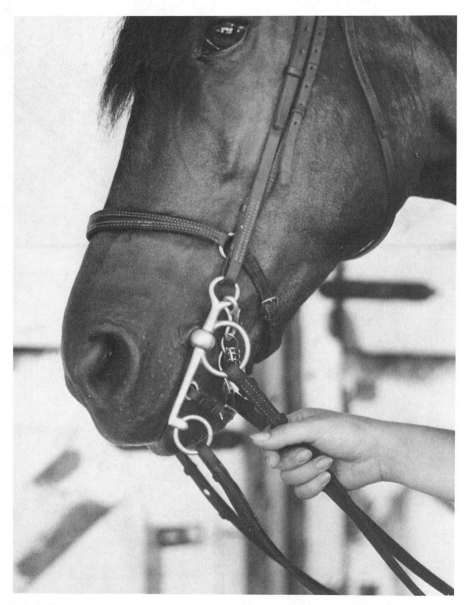

The Pelham-type bit combines the direct action of a snaffle with the lever action of a curb in a single bit.

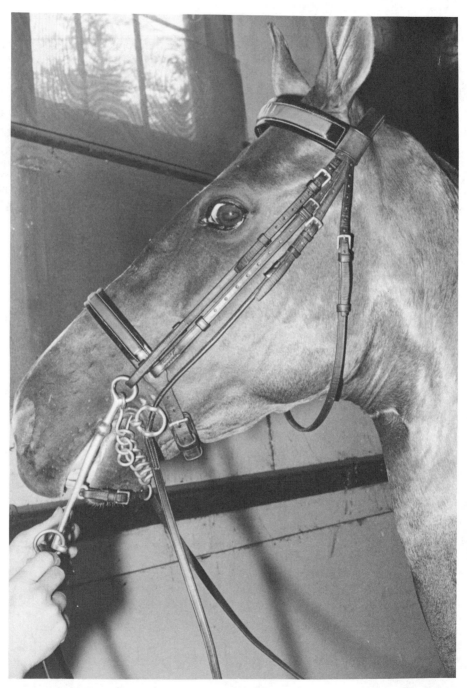

The gag snaffle is a bit designed for a special purpose. The rein and rounded cheek piece are continuous, providing a sort of pulley action to help raise a horse's head.

more control depends on the situation. But if the horse's responses (or his head carriage) are not what you want, a change of some kind is probably indicated. Sometimes just changing bits will work wonders. In other cases it is necessary to re-mouth the horse completely before you can correct bad habits that originated in the mouth.

Two approaches are commonly used to remake a horse's mouth. Unless the horse is seriously unmanageable so as to be dangerous to ride, many people prefer to develop the mouth through regular riding (or driving) depending on changed bits and communicative hands to effect gradual improvement in the horse's response.

The other method—which I prefer—is to treat the horse like a green colt that has never been trained. First, I give the horse a period of complete rest, preferably in pasture, to allow time for his memories of previous handling and bitting to fade.

I begin, then, with a gentle snaffle bit without reins and let the horse wear it in the stall for a couple of hours a day. At first I just want him to get used to the idea that the bit itself does not cause discomfort.

After a time, I begin putting on bitting harness, loosely adjusted. Usually, it will have a side check, to keep his head up, and side reins to begin teaching flexion. For the first few days the horse wears it for less than half an hour each day. Then, as time goes by, I begin adjusting the side reins or the check to apply light pressure (which the horse can relax by flexing properly).

When the horse is flexing to the bits and relaxing he is ready to begin exercising in bitting tack. Depending on circumstances, I may turn him out in a small paddock some days to exercise more or less at will and adjust himself to moving around with light contact on the bit. Other days I will lunge him to regulate the exercise and teach him to respond to simple commands to stop and start.

The work continues then with line driving and eventually saddle or harness work, usually in a single snaffle with running martingale.

A device that is particularly useful in preparing to make the transition from single snaffle to full bridle is a double-rein snaffle. As the name implies, it is a simple snaffle bridle with two pairs of reins. One pair comes directly from the bit to your hands and the other pair passes through a running martingale. The first pair gives you the usual snaffle action enabling you to steer him and raise his head. The reins that go through the martingale give you

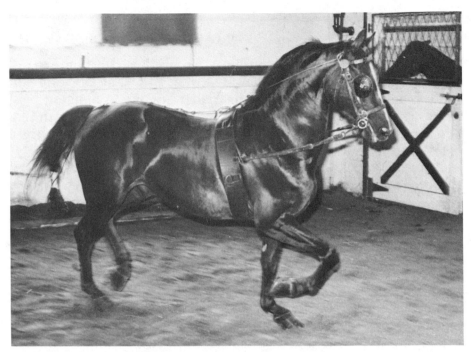

Turned loose in bitting tack, the horse can exercise at will and adjust himself to moving around with light contact on the bit.

After the horse has grown accustomed to wearing bitting tack, he can begin line driving. The handler directs the horse from behind but walks slightly to one side to avoid the possibility of being kicked.

As the horse progresses in bitting tack and long lines, the trainer can stay in the center of the circle and guide the horse around.

Draw rein arrangement enables the handler to vary the pressure of the side reins to achieve the desired degree of flexion.

some of the effect of a curb without the lever action on the mouth. They help to lower the horse's head and get him to flex at the poll.

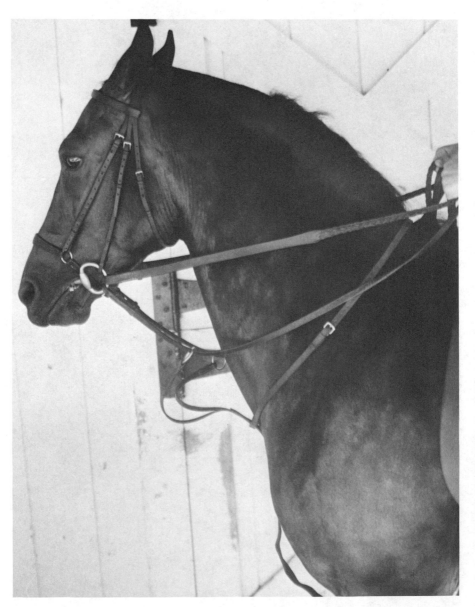

A double-rein snaffle is particularly useful in schooling green horses and retraining older ones. The upper rein provides direct action while the lower rein through the running martingale helps to develop flexion.

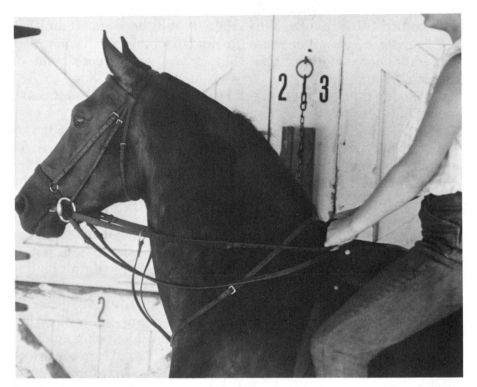

A common mistake: The double-rein snaffle incorrectly rigged with the martingale on the upper rein.

Some horses, in spite of this back-to-basics approach, will continue to give you problems that require additional attention. The suggestions that follow for dealing with some of the more common mouth-related habits are methods that get results in a reasonable number of cases. But, once again, horses are individuals. The techniques that work with one horse may not work with another. Variations and innovation may provide a better key to retraining your horse.

Pullers

The cure for the habit of pulling lies in the realization that there is no such thing as a one-ended tug-of-war. In other words, you don't break a horse of pulling by trying to outpull him. You do it by consistently refusing to pull against him.

Normally a horse should find that pulling on the reins causes discomfort in his mouth. Why, then, would he want to do it?

Logically, he does it because the mild discomfort in his mouth is preferable to something else that causes him greater fear or discomfort.

If you can figure what that something is, you're well on the way to solving the problem.

Most often, that something else was the way he was ridden by the person who owned him when he learned the habit. Picture, for instance, a rather inexpert rider whose seat was not very secure and who unwittingly used the reins as hand holds to stay in the saddle. The experience was likely to be most unsettling to the horse until he found that accepting a heavy hand on the reins would at least keep that oaf from flopping all over his back.

Or perhaps the person who taught him the habit was not so inexpert, but simply had heavy hands. If the horse didn't incline to take a firm hold of the bit, he was made to.

The cure, either way, is patient retraining. Little by little, let the horse have a looser rein. If he breaks gait, take back immediately, and when he settles down, begin loosening again.

Use intermittent pressure on the reins to signal him to turn or slow down. Never resort to a steady pull. Give rein to him when he tries to pull, and take back only briefly now and then, to check his speed.

Another very useful approach is to work the horse occasionally in different bits.

One other, rather different cause of pulling may be that the horse is underbitted for the work you are asking him to. He may, for instance, simply be too bold-moving for effective control in a simple snaffle or even a shortshank rubber Pelham. To correct pulling, it may be preferable to use bits that can give you more control than you actually need most of the time. Like the emergency brake on a car, they are there—rarely used—but available when needed.

Overbending

The opposite of the puller is the horse that avoids any pressure on the bit. He will flex until his chin touches his chest rather than accept a light touch on the reins.

The cause, quite likely, is quite similar to the cause of pulling. Both come from past experiences that caused pain or distress.

The habits are simply different ways of escaping from the same balanced equation.

The overbending horse needs to be worked in the gentlest kind of bridle. Quite often a hackamore is an excellent way to get him started. He should be encouraged to extend himself. Consistent work with light hands should bring gradual improvement as you build his confidence.

Tongue over Bit

A number of special bits are available for the horse that persists in putting his tongue over the bit. Before you go shopping for one, though, see if some simpler steps will get results.

First, examine his mouth for signs of soreness. He may have an injury that will heal if he is rested for awhile.

Make sure, also, that the bit you are using is wide enough and adjusted high enough in his mouth. A bit that hangs low—almost to the front teeth—invites the horse to put his tongue over it.

A snug noseband or cavesson is adequate in many cases to keep the horse's mouth closed and keep his tongue where it belongs.

A regular bit with a medium-high port will also discourage the habit by making it more difficult or uncomfortable to put the tongue over the bit than to keep it under.

Another effective trick is to tie a shoelace to the center of the port and bring the ends out either side of the horse's mouth and tie them on top of his nose.

Then in other cases—and in the similar problem of the horse who lets his tongue loll out the side of his mouth—the most effective method is to tie his tongue in place when you ride until the horse learns that keeping his tongue where it belongs reduces pain.

A patented rubber tongue tie is available in tack shops. But you can do just as well with a length of gauze or ribbon. Don't use cord or string, as this can cut the tongue. Use a broad enough strip of material to prevent injuring the tender tissues.

Form a loop in the strip with a simple overhand knot. Grasp the horse's tongue and put it through the loop so the knot is under the tongue and as high in the mouth as possible. Draw the loop tight and tie a second overhand knot over the first one—actually making it a square knot. Now bring the ends of the gauze out either side of his mouth and tie them securely under his chin.

A tongue tie should be used for only short periods of time. If it is tight enough to hold the tongue in position, it will be tight enough to restrict circulation in the tongue.

If half a dozen rides with one of these devices doesn't cure the habit, you can consider it a semipermanent part of the horse. At that point it is time to shop for one of those special bits that will keep the horse's tongue where you want it.

Head Tossing and Stargazing

Almost invariably these habits are caused by poor hands and bits that are too severe. Obviously, the horse would not adopt this ungainly, unnatural and uncomfortable way of going if something weren't bothering him.

Once the habit is ingrained, though, the horse may behave as if he is anything but overbitted. Nonetheless, begin your cure by changing to milder bits.

A martingale is also indicated to bring the horse's head down while you are conditioning him to the idea that a natural head carriage is not going to hurt the way it used to.

One-Sided Mouth

Occasionally you may encounter a horse that is more sensitive on one side of his mouth than the other. This of course, is either the result of some kind of accident which damaged the tissues on one side or the result of being ridden by someone who used his dominant hand (left or right) much more than the other.

Most riders, in fact, are slightly one-sided from being left- or righthanded. But the differences are usually slight. We also observe that horses have a discernible tendency to favor one side- —they prefer one lead at the canter or they tend to turn one way more readily than the other. We don't know whether horses, like people, are "right-handed" or whether they favor one side as a result of being trained by right-handed or left-handed people.

If the peculiarity in a horse is so pronounced that he pulls on one side or carries his head to one side, corrective measures are in order.

In her delightful book, *Jump for Joy*, Pat Smythe, one of the great international competitors of her generation, relates the story of a horse who was completely one-sided and quite unable to bend in the other direction. She initiated a correction by pulling his head way around in the direction he did not want to bend and tying it to his tail, then leaving him to thrash it out by himself. After an hour of fighting and throwing himself, he was wringing wet and exhausted. But after he was carefully cooled out he had learned that it did no good to fight against bending in that direction. With continued expert handling he became a great international jumper.

Another means of dealing with a one-sided mouth is to use a special bit. Remove one half of a jointed snaffle (the side on which the horse pulls) and replace that half of the mouthpiece with several links of smooth chain of the sort used for lead shanks. This will give you a training bit that will compensate for the unequal sensitivity in the horse's mouth. Or a similar result can be obtained by padding one side of the bit with latex tape and leaving the other side (the insensitive side) unpadded.

12
The Horse That Won't Walk

For pleasure riding in most parts of the country, you want a horse that walks willingly, because you spend a lot more time walking than doing any other gait. The horse that won't settle down and walk will exhaust himself and his rider, exasperate any other riders trying to keep up with him, and probably make you feel that your spine is being hammered halfway up into the back of your skull.

When you first learned to ride, you learned that pulling on the reins gave the horse a signal to stop, while loosening the reins gave him a cue to go. Much of the time this holds true. But when it comes to a horse that won't walk, pulling on the reins usually makes the problem worse.

To be more specific, if your horse wants to go faster than a walk—and this usually happens when he is headed back to the barn—taking a firm and unyielding hold on the reins does little good. The horse is trying to speed up because he wants to get to the barn where he expects to find food and security. Your restraint frustrates his natural desire for that security. And that frustration creates a nervous reaction that makes him need the security even more. So he tries even harder. He leans into the bit, prances and jiggles, giving you a most uncomfortable ride. In time this becomes his reaction to other situations that make him nervous.

Probably the most commonly tried cure for the horse that won't walk is one that almost never works. Countless inexperienced riders have reasoned that the horse will not walk because he is "feeling too good" and needs a couple of hours of work to settle him dowm. Trouble is, after a couple of hours of struggle, the high-strung horse is more nervous than ever, still jigging and fighting the bit, and the rider is so irritated he probably no longer cares whether the horse walks or not. He just wants to get off!

If "feeling too good" is really the reason why the horse is not walking (and occasionally this is the case) he will have the edge off in ten minutes or less. If he is still edgy after that, the problem calls for a different solution.

Horses that won't walk need a kind of handling that will reduce nervousness, stress, and anticipated discomfort. They have picked up the habit as a defense mechanism. As with all other similar patterns, it will yield best to patient retraining that delivers reinforcing rewards for doing the right thing.

First, pick a suitable location, preferably an enclosed ring or paddock, where the horse is in familiar surroundings and where he will not be stimulated to head for home at a more rapid pace.

Instead of trying to force the horse to walk, urge him up into the bridle and make him trot several times around the ring.

The rider should also make a conscious effort to relax as much as possible. Tension in your grip of the saddle communicates itself to the horse. He will feel your tension, and it will create a feeling of stress in him. So relax, but don't immediately ask the horse to walk if he isn't willing to.

It may sound confusing to say that you teach a horse to walk properly by *making* him trot. But, if you start out by trying to force him to walk, you will trigger his habitual defense, and he will be set on resisting you. Instead you want to establish some rapport with him. So, since he thinks he wants to trot, ask him to trot.

Let him go several times around the ring at the trot while you maintain a light but steady contact through the reins. Use intermittent leg pressure to urge him into the bridle and to encourage him to move at a brisk rate. Don't let him break into a gallop, but make him move right along.

When he has trotted steadily for several minutes, give him a

Give a signal to stop, sit easily in the saddle, and loosen your reins as soon as he begins to slacken his speed.

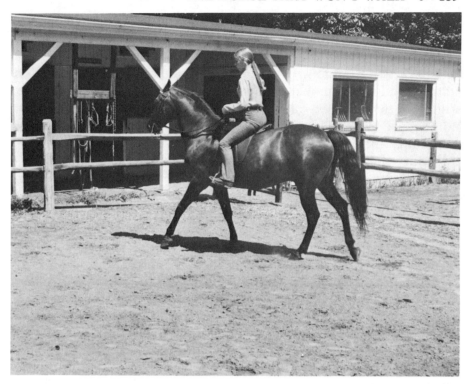

As long as he will walk quietly on a loose rein, let him; if he starts to jog, make him trot. *Repeat the sequence until he walks a reasonable distance, then reward him by putting him away.*

definite signal to slow down. Take up on the reins, say "whoa," sit down in the saddle and, *as soon as he slackens his pace*, begin loosening the reins. Relax your leg pressure, also. As he comes to a walk, let your reins fall noticeably looser than they were while you were trotting.

Your horse will probably walk a few steps, at least. He may then start to fuss and jog again. When he does, immediatley take up the reins and urge him into a trot as before. Again, don't try to force him to walk. The use of force makes him nervous, and nervousness makes him avoid walking.

After trotting another turn or two of the ring, repeat the request to walk. Loosen the reins as soon as he responds.

This time he may walk a little farther before he becomes restive again. As long as he walks, let him experience the absence of pressure from reins and legs. When he stops walking, give him distinct signals to trot once more.

Continue this way. When he will walk, *let* him; when he insists on jogging, *make* him.

Usually, by the fifth or sixth time you ask him to slow to a walk he will be experiencing a distinct difference between stress when he trots and freedom when he walks. As that difference becomes apparent to him he will walk an appreciably longer distance. When he does, it's time to end lesson number one. Stop him, dismount, and put him away.

Be sure that his *last* experience for this lesson is one of walking flat and relaxed. For that reason, don't chance riding him back to the barn. He's almost certain to be too eager to get there to walk the distance.

When you start out the next day it may seem that he has forgotten the first lesson entirely. That's normal. But after a week or so he should be walking much more willingly.

When he seems to understand what is wanted from the distinctly different signals for walking and trotting, use the same system to teach him to canter and walk alternately on command. As soon as this is going well, you are ready to let him try it outside the familiar ring where he has been working.

Avoid paths and situations that will breed excitement and uneasiness at first. Take him out for short rides, alternately walking and trotting. When he *won't* walk, *make* him trot. But always finish up by walking the last quarter mile back to the barn.

That should be a strict rule with any horse you ride. He should never be allowed to approach the barn at any gait faster than a walk. Failing to observe this rule not only allows a horse to develop a habit of refusing to walk but can also encourage runaways. Whether that last distance is exactly a quarter mile is not vital. It can be more or less. But you should fix in your mind a suitable point in each direction that makes the boundary of your own "walking zone." Insist that the horse only walk inside this area. The entrance to your front lane or driveway would be a very logical limit, for instance.

The barn-sour horse is a specialized version of the horse that won't walk. He is the one that will walk readily enough any time you ask him—*except* that last quarter mile back to the barn. He probably got that way because someone let him run for home at the end of his rides.

He may require a different method of retraining. As the barn comes in sight and he quickens his pace, turn him in a circle and head him back the other way until he settles to a walk again. Then start him for home once more. Each time he speeds up, turn him away until he gets the idea that the only he can get to the barn is by walking on a loose rein. It can take an exasperatingly long time. But in the interest of safety, the effort is worth it.

13
The Horse That Won't Back

Properly mouthed and bitted, a horse should rein back almost as readily as he moves forward. Some, though, have never learned to. And others have been conditioned to expect backing to mean that they will be yanked on and they consequently learn to raise their heads and plant themselves in defense.

In order to back correctly, the horse must flex and lower his head. He needs to adjust his center of gravity to take weight off his hindquarters. Neither of those requisites is possible if the rider leans back (putting more weight over the rear quarter) and pulls roughly on the bit, forcing the horse to raise his head.

If, when you ask a horse to back, he starts to set himself with head up and weight to the rear, immediately loosen your reins and move him forward a step or two. When his head drops and he flexes, gently use a give-and-take motion on the reins to ask him to back. Repeating this sequence three or four times will often be enough to get him to back a step or two if his habit is not too deeply ingrained.

If it works, and he does back, even a very short distance, it is my practice to stop immediately, dismount, and put him away. Or, if his work for the day is not finished, I will not ask him to back again that day. He should learn that cooperation in any degree brings relief from the stress that was troubling him.

I once had an old Saddlebred horse that was an ideal mount for equitation riders. He was really a "push button" horse. If the rider could just stay in the middle of his back, the horse would quite

In order to back correctly, the horse must flex and lower his head. He needs to adjust his center of gravity to take weight off his hindquarters.

If your horse sets himself with head up and weight to the rear, immediately loosen your reins and move him forward a step or two.

literally do his gaits on the ringmaster's commands.

He was foolproof, too, on all the usual equitation figures. The one thing he was not always perfect about was backing. He would do it, if you didn't ask him too often. But if the students who rode him tried to practice backing several times in one lesson, he would plant himself and refuse to back.

Because of this, I had to made it a rule that he was only backed once a day—at the end of a lesson. With that routine, backing was always the last thing he did before he returned to the barn. As long as I stuck to that rule we had no trouble.

With more stubborn cases, it is common practice to have an assistant stand in front of the horse while you ask him to back. If the horse does not respond, the assistant tries to scare him or, perhaps, uses a whip on his front legs to drive him backward.

None of this is calculated to relieve his fear and develop his sense of security. It may teach him to back away from someone who stands in front of him with a whip. But there is a much better way to make use of an assistant.

Your helper should have a rope shank at least three or four feet long. Holding the rope with both hands about two feet apart, he puts the rope over the horse's nose a little below the midway point between eyes and nostrils. Then, as you ask the horse to back, your helper pulls alternately with either hand in a sort of "sawing" motion.

Without creating panic, or causing pain as you would be pulling on the bits, this method provides a pressure that the horse wants to move away from. Few, indeed, are stubborn enough to get a rope burn from refusing to back when this method is applied.

As soon as the horse backs, the assistant should withdraw the rope. At the same time the rider should pat the horse, ride him around for a few minutes, and then ask him to back again. If the horse does not do it, the assistant should repeat the application of the rope. Continue this way until the horse backs without the rope. When he does, dismount and put him away.

A large percentage of horses will back after one such lesson. Some need a second lesson. In rare cases it may take a third. I have never known a horse that needed more than three sessions of this kind to understand that backing when asked to is painless.

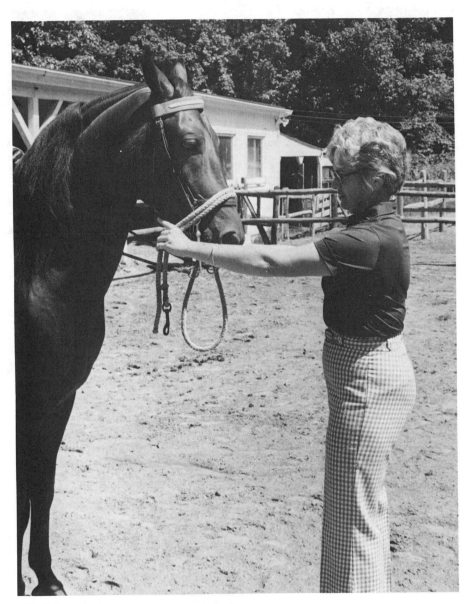

Have your assistant hold a length of rope over the horse's nose.

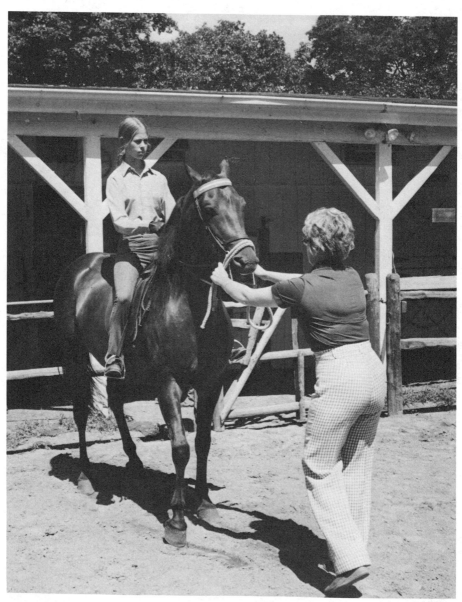

As you ask the horse to back, your assistant pulls the rope back and forth over the horse's nose in a sawing motion.

14
The Horse That Is Hard to Mount

The best way to begin with a horse that is hard to mount is to start the lessons in a confined area where he can't go far if he moves off while you are getting into the saddle. If there is sufficient headroom in his stall, it would be an ideal place to practice. It is not only confined, but it is a place of security for the horse.

If there is no suitable place inside your barn, a small, familiar paddock, away from distractions, will do almost as well. A fence corner is good, too, where you can place the horse with his right side against one fence and with his head facing directly at the other. That will prevent him from moving forward or away from you as you mount.

Whatever spot you have picked, begin slowly and quietly. Take plenty of time. Speak to the horse soothingly until he settles down and relaxes. Gather up your reins in your left hand. Make them short enough so that you'll have control when you get aboard, but not so tight that you are pulling on his mouth while you are mounting.

Rest your left hand (with the reins) on his neck. Pause and let him settle again if he seems to be anticipating your next move. Then quietly turn the near stirrup with your right hand and hold it while you raise your left foot to the stirrup.

Some horses will take this move as the signal to start fussing. You may have to repeat it several times before he will stand still while you're in that awkward position with one foot in the stirrup and the other on the ground. When he does stand, move your right

Place the horse in a confined area, such as a fence corner, so that he can't move away from you as you mount.

hand to the cantle of the saddle and, in one smooth move, step up and swing into the saddle.

Modify the details of this procedure to suit your own capabilities and to find what is least upsetting to your horse. But concentrate on getting him accustomed to the routine in a way that will relieve his fears.

Don't make any one day's lesson last too long. When you have made your point, stop. Repeating the drill too many times without giving the horse a direct reward for doing well will not improve his learning. It is better to give him an immediate reward when he stands relatively well for mounting. The best reward for a horse in a situation he fears is to remove the cause of the fear. So, at the beginning, if he stands reasonably well once or twice, remove the tack and put him away.

As his willingness improves, you can begin riding a short distance after you mount. One turn of the yard or once around the

Gather the reins in your left hand and place the hand on the horse's withers. Use your right hand to steady your stirrup as you prepare to mount.

ring should be the maximum the first time or two. Remember, you want to condition him to the idea that being mounted does not lead to other unpleasant tasks or consequences. Continue to reward him by not asking more of him than simple acceptance of mount-

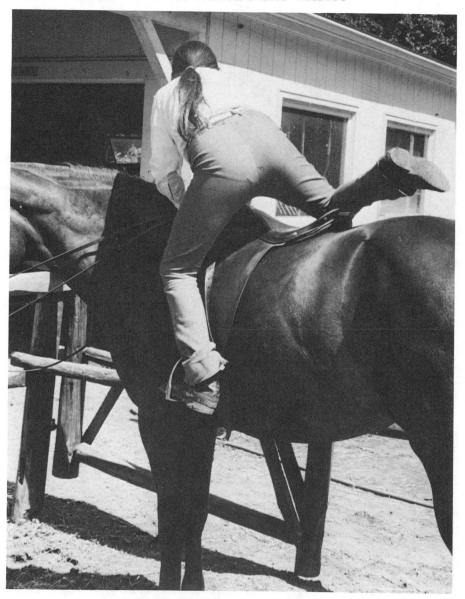

Swing up into the saddle with one smooth move.

ing. If all goes well, your patience will be rewarded with distinct improvement within a week. And that week invested in asking nothing more of him may lead to years of dependable enjoyment.

While many horses will respond to this process of simple reconditioning, a few special measures may help with the more stubborn (i.e., more frightened) individuals. Blinkers, for instance, may be very helpful in some cases. They probably won't help with the horse whose bad habit takes the form of being too eager to take off when you mount. But they may help a lot with the

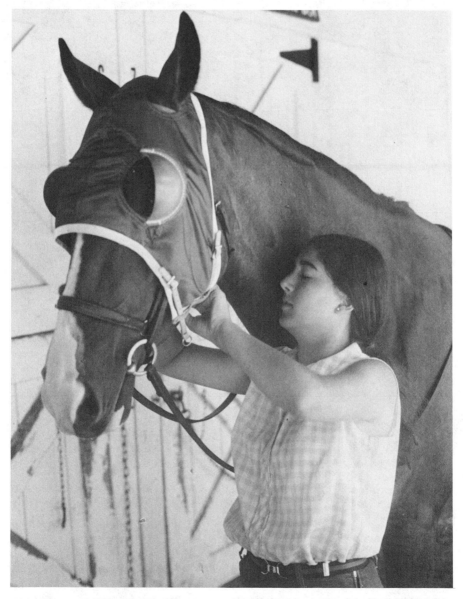

Blinkers may help with a horse that is frightened by someone climbing on his back. The blinkers cut off the optical alarm effect of motions behind his head.

The horse will learn to accept mounting if you have a helper to hold his head and feed him a treat just as you swing into the saddle.

horse whose reflexes are triggered by your movements in his peripheral field of vision.

There are several ways that having an assistant to work with you can be very helpful. One is to have the person stand in front of the horse to steady him and give him a treat to eat just as you mount. This will distract the horse's attention from the thing he fears and will also reward him for doing what you want.

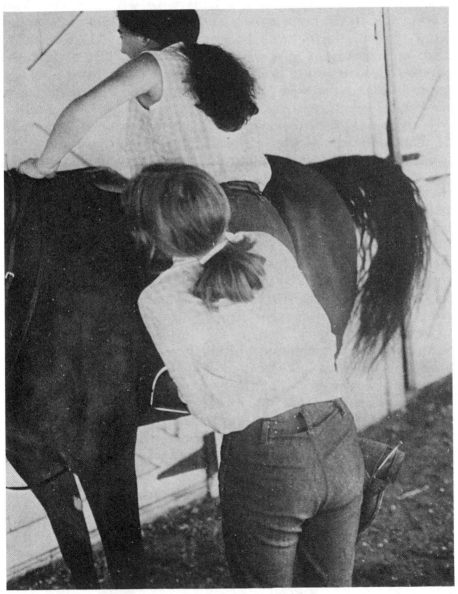

Having an assistant to give you a "leg up" is often a help with a horse that won't stand for mounting.

Another way the assistant might help is to give you a "leg up"—particularly valuable with a tall horse if you have some difficulty getting into the saddle with that "one smooth movement" we talked about.

If your helper is delegated to hold the horse's head while you mount, be sure he holds the bridle by the cheek pieces or noseband, *not by the reins or bits*. Otherwise, what happens? You start to mount, the horse moves a little, the assistant pulls on the bit to stop him, the bit hurts the horse's mouth, and he throws his head up looking for an escape from the pain just as you are completing your swing into the saddle. It adds up to a totally unpleasant situation with fear of pain associated with mounting in the horse's memory.

The general rule is to leave the horse's mouth alone, so long as he stands, until you are in the saddle, but to have the reins collected enough to exert control if necessary. That, however, was the wrong answer for a horse I encountered some years ago. He had been specifically trained to stand if the reins were resting on his neck and to move off as soon as the reins were picked up. If you tried to gather your reins to mount him, you'd be going at a strong gallop by the time your seat hit the saddle. But if you left the reins untouched on his neck, he would stand stock still until you mounted and picked up the reins. Discovering this idiosyncrasy of someone else's training saved immeasurable hours of effort and immediately transformed a problem horse into a solid citizen.

Another useful technique with the horse that is too anxious to head for the distant hills is called "cheeking." Gather your reins in the left hand as usual, but instead of resting your hand on the horse's neck in the usual way, reach forward and catch the throat latch or cheek pieces of the bridle and draw the horse's head toward you as you mount. Then, if the horse does move while you are mounting, he can only move toward you and turn in a tight circle.

15
The Runaway

Nothing is more frightening and few things are more dangerous than the runaway. A horse that takes off at top speed and resists all efforts to bring him under control is a serious menace.

The speed itself is not the problem. A fast-running horse is easy to sit. But the blind panic of the horse that runs away will carry him heedless into any number of dangers. Runaways will dash into fast-moving traffic on the highway, smash through fences, careen into buildings, or rush onto unsafe footing leading to a fall.

I was once asked to ride a horse who had the nasty habit of running back to the barn. Forewarned, I thought I was forearmed. I was prepared to stop him from breaking into a gallop as we returned from a short ride. Prepared, yes, but unsuccessful. When he was ready to go, he went regardless of precautions.

I had prepared a fall-back position in case my first plan didn't work. To return to the barn, the horse had to make a right-angle turn to the left into the lane. I was sure that if I could prevent that turn so that he had to pass the entrance, I would be able to stop him. So, as he neared the gate, I slid my right hand down the off rein, almost to the bit, and braced myself to keep him from turning his head.

The thing I hadn't counted on happened. The right rein broke off neatly, leaving me with a handful of nothing. He made the turn and accelerated still more, taking dead aim on the small barn door which was high enough for him but not for me. I sensed the certainty of skull fracture and the possibility of decapitation if he went through that door at the speed he was going. I'll never know why he stopped dead, inches from my doom, with his head inside the door and the rest of him—and me—parked outside.

Since then I have never tried to work with a runaway in any but controlled surroundings. It is simply too dangerous.

Under unusual circumstances the most dependable horse may bolt if something frightens him. Another example from personal experience: There was a very sensible horse that I had been jogging in harness to limber him up after a long trailer ride to a horse show. I was starting to unhook him, and when I released the check rein the horse shook his head in the harmless way that horses sometimes do. He happened to shake it in just the right way and shook the bridle off altogether. It startled him, as you might imagine. Suddenly free of the blinkers, he caught sight of the cart behind him and jumped to get away. But, since he was still hooked, the cart followed. In three more steps he was traveling at a dead run. By the time he stopped, he had smashed the jog cart (slamming it against a car) torn up the harness, and given himself another two miles of exercise around the fairgrounds track.

That wasn't a question of a bad habit. It was an accident that might happen with any horse. And to prove the point, I showed him that night in harness and placed in the ribbons.

A persistent runaway, on the other hand, is one who has learned it as a defense. It usually begins with a fear situation. The most natural thing for a horse to do is run away from something he fears.

It could start with almost any kind of frightening event. An inexperienced rider takes a horse for a ride. Something startling happens—a passing truck backfires, a yapping dog runs out and nips at the horse's heels, or perhaps another rider gallops past without warning. It need not be a volcano erupting. Just something that sparks a beginning fear reaction. The horse begins to bolt, scaring the rider.

Now the cycle is self-renewing. The rider's fear is communicated to the horse through hands, seat, voice, and every point of contact. It makes the horse more afraid and he runs faster, which makes the rider more afraid, and so on.

Conditioned once with this sequence of events, the horse's brain establishes a path which makes the same thing happen more readily the next time. A few such episodes and a classic habit is established. From then on, it won't matter much who rides him. He is likely to bolt if something startles him.

In time, a stronger, more secure rider can decondition the horse and change the pattern. But it does take time—and a considerable element of risk.

THE RUNAWAY • 177

The runaway reflex can be acquired in other ways. It is not always inspired by unexpected fright. Many horses have actually been taught to run out of control by foolish owners. They have learned that a certain signal means they are expected to head out at top speed. And there are the horses who quite naturally quickened their step as they neared home at the end of the ride and found that their riders were perhaps not skilled enough to slow them down. First they came home at a jog, and the next time they came at a faster trot, and the next time at a gallop...until they were regularly hitting the barnyard at a dead run.

Of all the horses I've ever handled, perhaps the most embarrassing was a Thoroughbred hunter who had previously been a successful race horse. He learned early in life that when a male rider (such as a jockey) took a firm hold on the reins, he was expected to turn on his speed.

Long retired from the track, he was docile—a delightful ride for any woman or child who gave him a loose rein. But let a man get on his back and take a little hold of his mouth, and there was no stopping him until he had run himself to a standstill. Try as I might, I never found a way to change him. Some horses just aren't curable.

A horse with a known proclivity for running away should be approached with the utmost care. To provide any basis for further correction, I recommend going back to basics. With the lunge line, bitting tack and long lines, proceed to teach the horse to respond to *your* commands to stop, turn, and start as if he had never been taught before. With each handler there are slight differences in the way the aids are used. You want the horse thoroughly trained to respond to you and the subtleties in your handling so there can be no mistaking the communication you transmit to him.

If your horse does not learn to stop promptly in response to your command and to remain perfectly still until your signal to move, he may need a few lessons with the safety rigging, which is a variation of the "running W." For this purpose, it should never be used to trip or throw the horse. That would only create an unnecessary element of fear. But when he is working on the lunge, signal him to stop and tighten the safety line just enough to apply a positive restraint. This done correctly, he will be able to stand without falling, but he won't be able to continue moving.

Only when he stops reliably on your signal should you consider working him under saddle (or in harness). Then, for a time, all riding should be within an enclosed area. Continue to school him on starting, turning, and stopping on your command. Study his response to the bits you are using and make any changes that seem necessary. There is a great tendency to bit runaways with increasingly severe hardware: long shank curbs, wire curb chains, draw reins, dropped nosebands. If a way could be found to attach hydraulic brakes, I'm sure someone would try them. While any horse should be adequately bitted, training is what is needed. Extremely harsh equipment may stop the horse, but probably won't break the bad habit. Habits are broken by training; jaws are broken by pulleys and gimmicks.

If you have done the groundwork and retraining thoroughly, your horse may never try to run with you. More likely, the day will come when he will try. When that time comes, you should be prepared with some ways of stopping him.

First, of course, don't panic or freeze on the reins. One thing that almost never works is just pulling hard on the reins. In a state of panic or precalculated rebellion, the horse will simply brace himself against you and run all the harder.

Better results may be had if you get a firm grip in the saddle, lean forward and give him his head for a moment, then take back hard. When he slackens speed a little, give him his head again and repeat. Two or three times and this unexpected treatment will stop many horses.

To run at full speed, a horse must be able to lower and extend his neck. Getting his head up will help get him under control. It may not stop him, but it will keep him from taking complete control and it will improve your chances of gaining mastery of the situation. For this reason, a war bridle is sometimes useful as a kind of emergency brake.

A runaway usually has picked the direction he wants to go. If you can change his direction you will diminish his ambition to run. Where space permits, a runaway can be stopped by turning him in ever smaller circles. Eventually he will have to stop to avoid falling down.

One other recommended method is this: Get a firm, short grip on one rein, low beside the neck. Then bring the other rein over the neck and lean your weight on it. This is the method used by race-track riders to pull up horses that are far too strong to be controlled by a direct pull on the reins.

16
The Balker

The opposite problem from the runaway is the balker—the horse that will stop dead and refuse to move. It was not an uncommon problem with carriage horses a hundred years ago. But a genuine balker is rare these days.

Let's separate the horse who stops for an obvious reason from the true balker whose stubborn refusal to move is not related to any of his immediate surroundings. A horse who refuses a jump, or one who won't ford a stream, is not strictly speaking a balker. He is making a direct response to some stimulus that causes insecurity. He is unwilling to do what you ask because the task frightens him.

The balker is another matter. He will stop for no apparent reason, and will endure considerable urging or even punishment rather than move on.

It is a habit that is hard to relate to the usual balanced equation where fear of punishment equals fear of doing what is asked of him. It is a reaction that is more neurotic and the means of curing it is therefore harder to find.

I was judging a major horse show recently where I watched one horse come quite suddenly to a standstill and refuse to move another step. Up until then he had been going along nicely. Nothing unusual had happened to cause him to balk. He just stopped and wouldn't budge.

I have no way of telling why he did it. But I had the distinct impression that it was his way of saying, "This excitement is just too much for me. I give up!"

And that would be typical of the other balkers I have encountered. They seem to reach some kind of breaking point that is entirely internal. They give no outward sign that it is coming until suddenly they are standing still and nothing you do will make them move.

In one of the most entertaining books in which horses are a significant element in the plot, a balker helped David Harum get even with The Deacon, his horse-trading rival (*David Harum*, by W.N. Westcott). At the start, though, it seemed that the hero had been neatly taken.

David was warned in advance that a certain horse "would stand without hitching." This, it turned out, was a euphemisn to conceal the fact that the horse had a habit of balking.

Discovering the horse's fault, David dealt with it this way. When the horse balked, Harum gave him one lick on the shoulder with the buggy whip. The horse didn't move. So the canny horse trader got out of the buggy, and using an assortment of miscellaneous buckles and straps, he tied the horse up so he *couldn't* move. Then he waited until the horse decided he wanted to move along and found out that he was totally restrained.

David repeated the whole procedure on several occasions until the horse got the idea that if he didn't move when he got that tap on the shoulder from the whip, he wouldn't be able to move when *he* wanted to.

The story is fiction, of course. But it suggests that outthinking a balker will get better results than losing your temper and trying to make him move by breaking a whip over his back. Severe punishment simply does not get results with a stubborn balker.

Better than punishment is some kind of persuasion that will get him moving—in any direction at all, and one that will get his mind off this particular pattern of rebellion.

Some years ago I had a saddle pony to train. He was about as badly spoiled as a horse could get. He would not only stop whenever he felt like it, but would rear if any effort was made to make him move. From what I could piece together of his history he had alternately been in the hands of children who could not make him behave and trainers who had been overly abusive.

It was slow progress trying to win his confidence and cooperation. The only way to do it was by patiently, consistently and calmly taking him through basic training. I had him long enough to see some improvement, but his owners grew impatient and sold him before I had a chance to finish the job.

When the horse you are riding stops, you quite naturally apply heels and whip to urge him forward. It doesn't work. What then?

Many horses that won't move forward can be made to back up.

If the horse balks and refuses to move forward, the best approach is to get him moving in any direction.

Doing that vigorously might get the horse to forget his original intention and move forward willingly when the backing is over.

Some authorities even suggest backing the horse until he runs into something that will startle him and make him want to move forward. It can be effective—although I had one mare that balked, and this did not work at all. When she stopped, I backed her up until she hit the door of a greenhouse that happened to be nearby. She not only hit it, she smashed through it backward and still refused to move forward.

With exaggerated use of reins and leaning your weight to one side, the balker can be forced to turn, and this can start him moving.

Most often you can force the horse to make some move by turning him one way or another. Pull his head way around to one side and lean in that direction yourself. You can usually shift his center of gravity enough that he has to move his feet to keep from falling down. As soon as he takes a step in the direction you have turned him, turn him the other way and force another step in that direction. Most horses will become enough involved (or confused) by this procedure to forget their original intention and continue down the trail.

If your balker plants himself too solidly for that, try dismounting and leading him. If he won't go forward, turn him. You might even take the reins over his head, hold the reins short in your left hand, and as you pull his head toward you, grab his tail and spin him in two or three small circles. It is almost guaranteed to get his mind off balking for a while.

Just before the turn of this century, Captain O. R. Gleason was one of several intinerant showmen who billed themselves as "The

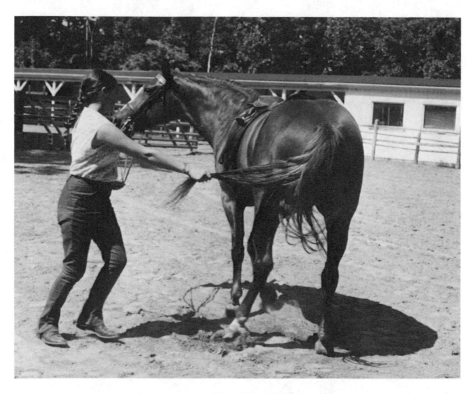

Another way to get a balker moving is to pull his head around to one side, grab his tail, and spin him in two or three small circles.

World's Greatest Horse Trainer.'' He traveled about the country giving shows to demonstrate his ability to deal with all kinds of problem horses. In a book on his methods, Gleason suggested that the best way to get a balker moving was to stand beside his

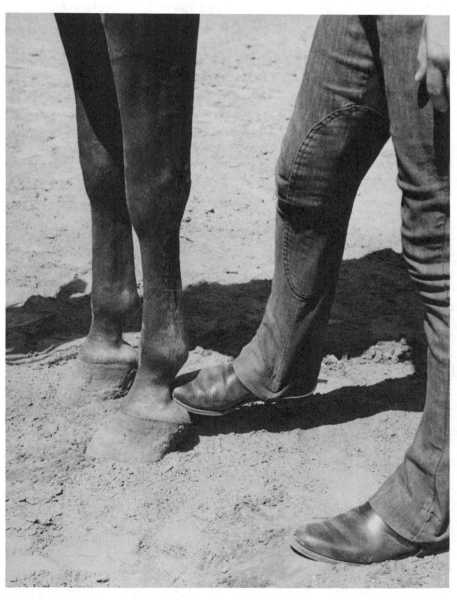

A sharp kick under the fetlock is one suggested method to make a balker start moving.

shoulder and with the toe of your boot give him a sharp kick in the back of the pastern below the fetlock.

Whatever device you hit on, the secret is to get the horse's mind off his resistance and start him moving. Balking is a fixation that does not yield to the *usual* methods of motivating forward impulsion. Its solution—and permanent cure—lies in finding an *unusual* motivation, a different method that works to get him started.

Our language is a trifle richer thanks to an idiom that originated in a probably apocryphal solution to balking. When we speak of motivating someone, we use the expression "building a fire under him."

17
Refusing to Jump

William Steinkraus, Olympic Gold Medalist and President of the United States Equestrian Team, makes the point that the art of jumping consists primarily of putting the horse into a position where he can make the jump. Then, in most cases, he will jump.

When a horse refuses, it is usually because he thinks he can't clear the jump. He is afraid of it. Or he may be afraid of the jab in the mouth he anticipates if his rider is not very secure in the saddle. And, in a good many cases, he senses his rider's subconscious fear and figures that if you are afraid, he should be too.

Horses develop the habit of refusing from being asked to jump too high, too soon, and too often. Like any other athletic feat, jumping requires the development of muscles and coordination. If the horse's ability is allowed to develop gradually, progressing from low, easy jumps to higher and more difficult ones only as he is ready for the next level, the horse is more likely to jump willingly. But if he is rushed before he is ready, he will soon be rapping his legs on the jumps and deciding that this flying business is for the birds. So he begins refusing, not only the jumps that are too tough for him but easier ones as well. (He wasn't born yesterday! He knows that if he takes a three-foot jump you'll raise the bar and make him try three feet six inches.)

Overcoming the habit of refusing requires going back to simpler, easier jumps for a while and re-establishing his proficiency. It is advisable to give the horse several days of working under saddle with no attempt at jumping. Then, after a ride, try just one or two low jumps and put the horse away after he takes them.

Most top trainers exercise their horses daily to keep them in condition, but they school over fences only once or twice a week—or less. Overschooling leads to problems such as habitual refusals.

In some cases, the horse who has adopted refusing as a defense will have to be taken all the way back to such beginning lessons as stepping over a rail on the ground and then gradually trained to jump again.

If inept riding has contributed to the habit, it is sometimes useful to get the horse started again by lunging him over jumps for a while before attempting to ride him over them.

Remember that at any stage in his training there is a practical limit to how high a horse can—or will—jump. Breaking the refusal habit depends on not exceeding that limit.

Only a few horses have the build, coordination, and athletic ability for really big fences. Not every prospect will make it to the Puissance events. Recognize your horse's limitations Expecting more of him than he is able to do leads to refusals and other escape mechanisms.

If the horse has been soured on jumping by inept riding, it is a good idea to get the horse jumping again by lunging over low obstacles until he regains his confidence.

Follow the work on the lunge line with a period of riding over low easy jumps until the horse has a chance to realize that he won't be pushed beyond his ability and won't be jabbed in the mouth by an insecure rider.

There are horses, too, who will refuse jumps within their ability because of other factors and stresses. I used to show a mare who was a capable and willing jumper. But she had the annoying habit of stopping to examine the first fence in any class she entered. I suspect the excitement of the occasion and the strange surroundings awakened her instinctive wariness, and refusing once was her way of reacting to the insecurity.

The solution with her was found in making her more concerned with pleasing her rider than she was about the unfamiliar situation. Chastising her for stopping was the right thing in this case. But this would have been wrong if I had been asking her to take jumps she was afraid of, or ones that were beyond her ability.

A good way to keep a horse jumping willingly—once you have established how high he *can* jump—is to limit your schooling to obstacles a little lower than he can actually handle. Concentrate on getting the horse to approach and take off correctly. If he does that well, and takes three foot six inch jumps consistently, another six inches won't make much difference when you need to jump four feet.

18
The Horse That Rears

Two sure "cures" are generally suggested for a horse that rears. One of them is to hit the horse between the ears when he starts to rear, with the butt of a riding crop, a lead pipe, or some similar weapon. It is even suggested that if you can break a bottle of water over his head you will surely end the bad habit. The other remedy suggested is to pull the horse over backward and hold him down while he meditates on his sins.

Without challenging the possible effectiveness of these solutions, we simply ask how many riders are agile enough to do any of these things? If you are, and you have a horse that rears, perhaps you will find them useful.

For most riders with a problem horse, there is difficulty enough in trying to stay on a rearing horse and at the same time keep him from falling backward on top of you. So perhaps there is a better way to deal with a rearer. If you take a problem-solving approach, you will first look for the reasons why the horse rears. Dealing with the cause rather than the result is the most constructive practice.

Classically, the horse turns to rearing as a defense against a stress situation. Reducing the stress usually reduces the horse's inclination to rear.

But, turning to specifics, it is useful to recognize that there is no way a horse can rear when he is moving forward. He has to stop, plant himself, and exert considerable muscular effort to lift about two thirds of his own weight, plus yours, off the ground. Rearing takes a lot more effort than moving forward. So if you can give the horse the alternative of moving away from the negative stimulus instead of rearing, you give him (and yourself) an easier way out.

In an earlier chapter I mentioned a mare that had developed a nasty habit of rearing as a means of getting out of working. Whenever she decided she had gone far enough, she would rear and the timid owner would let her go home. The rides got progressively shorter until she would not even go to the end of the driveway.

In dealing with the problem, I first took time to get acquainted with the mare in the ring at home. Finding that I had no trouble with her, I was ready to test her out on the road. Sure enough, before she had gone a mile, she stopped, wheeled and started back to the barn. When I tried to turn her back she reared.

Giving her a loose rein and a hearty thump in the ribs with my heels, I got her started again. Within a hundred yards she was ready to try again. This time I noticed that when she stopped, she consistently turned to the left. The normal reaction, of course, would be to immediately pull on the right rein to make her stay straight. That is what I had done when she reared. So this time, instead, I pulled on the *left* rein when she turned left, taking advantage of her own momentum and swinging her a full 360 degrees so that she was again heading away from home and moving forward.

Perhaps that mare wasn't very smart. After no more than three or four attempts that always ended the same way—still heading away from the barn, she gave up trying. The rearing problem vanished.

In that experience there is a clue that works with a lot of horses that try to rear. Again, they have to stop to rear. Getting them moving again is the best possible preventive for rearing. And in a lot of cases it is easier to get them turning than it is to get them moving forward. So, by wheeling in a circle you can often prevent them from rearing.

Another trainer suggests that you can discourage rearing this way: If the horse rears, give him a loose rein and lean forward. As the horse comes down, grab one of his ears, twist it, and wheel him in a tight circle. This is an appropriate kind of punishment that requires less special agility than such stunts as hitting the horse over the head when he rears, or pulling him over and sitting on him.

19
The Horse That Bucks

Just as forward motion is the effective key to preventing rearing, there is one way to stop a horse from bucking. A horse cannot really buck as long as his head is up. If his neck is horizontal or higher so that his ears are no lower than his withers, he can make a sudden leap (forward or sideways) and he can kick out with his back feet. But he can't buck with the kind of motion that will unseat any reasonably secure rider.

In order to buck, he needs to arch his backbone, and that is mechanically impossible when his head is elevated.

To stop a horse from bucking, then, all you really need to do is get his head up.

That's easy to say but under some circumstances not so easy to do. A horse that uses bucking as a means to escape from a situation doesn't give much warning that he is going to do it. He can have you completely off balance before you realize that you need to get his head up. If he is sneaky and you are unlucky, he can have you off before you can do anything to stop him.

This is one bad habit where it doesn't usually help much to understand why the horse behaves this way. Most horses buck because they don't want to be ridden. They want to get the rider off their backs. Of course you can't get bucked off if you don't get on. But this is a habit where an approach other than removing the cause will probably be your solution.

Not always. Some years ago I trained a young stud who progressed nicely through the usual stages in bitting tack, long lines, and he even started driving nicely in harness. The time came when I decided he was ready to be ridden. So I put on the saddle and the bridle which I prefer for starting colts. It has one snaffle bit, but

192

A horse must lower his head and arch his back in order to buck. To stop him, it is necessary to get his head up. Courtesy of Madison Square Garden.

two pairs of reins, one of which passes through a running martingale.

With the colt rigged this way, I took him out and lunged him a few minutes to let him get used to the unfamilar trappings, especially the stirrups flapping against his sides. I noticed that he seemed to be ducking his head a little, but it didn't seem important. Then, with an assistant holding the lunge line—for "safety" — I climbed aboard and asked him to move. Move he did! He dropped his head and went to bucking like a rodeo star. He dumped me unceremoniously into a bed of daffodils.

The next time I was ready when he tried it, so he didn't get me off. But he gave me exactly two choices. He was willing to stand still with me in the saddle. But the only kind of moving he would do was bucking.

Somehow I made a lucky guess—something about the way he

was ducking and fussing on the lunge line. On a hunch, I removed the running martingale, and *that* solved the whole problem. As soon as I tried to ride him with that slight change in tack—just a single rein—he became willing to walk and trot like a veteran. I will never know why he disliked that martingale, but a thing as small as that solved his bucking problem.

In general, horses with a naturally high head carriage (such as Arabians, Morgans, and Saddlebreds) have very little tendency to resort to bucking to solve their problems. If they do, they are not very good at it. Horses that typically carry a lower head, with neck extended more horizontally (typical of Quarter Horses, Appaloosas, and Thoroughbreds, for instance) have more bucking ability and seem more inclined to use it. The wild western Mustang is king of them all when it comes to the ability and tendency to buck.

In dealing with any horse that bucks we give first priority to fitting him with a bridle that gives maximum advantage in raising his head. For the time being we will forgo progress on other points of development and training until we can make sure that the bucking habit is abandoned. When that's done we can go back to another type of bridle if necessary.

For our purpose we will need a direct-action snaffle bit, probably a relatively sharp one (i.e., show bridoon, twisted mouth, or "knife edge") and possibly a gag snaffle or overcheck. Or we may use whatever snaffle is handy but increase its head-raising capability by attaching a shoelace that goes from one ring of the bit, over the gum under the horse's upper lip, to the other ring.

We can expect the horse to try bucking when a certain combination of factors produces fear and stress. The horse has a strong desire to get out of doing something you are urging him to do. You can equip him with your antibucking bits and wait for this to happen. Or you can create the situation and tempt him to try.

Either way, you want to be ready when he drops his head and starts to arch his back and pitch. Set yourself in the saddle and clamp your legs to his sides. At the same time reach forward as far as you can and pull up—hard—on the snaffle. Give him a sharp vocal reprimand at the same time.

Note that it is important to reach forward, shortening the rein as you do so, and give a sharp pull upward. Just pulling back on the snaffle will not get the horse's head up, which is what you must do.

If your effort succeeds, the horse will most likely come to a tense standstill. The escape route he depended on was cut off. It did not work. So he stops to consider another. This is the time to increase his sense of security—before his feeling of stress launches him into something else—or another try at bucking. Speak to him gently, stroke him and try to relax him.

That tense moment after he stops is critical. It is definitely not the time to punish him for bucking. It is never a good idea to punish a horse after he has stopped doing something wrong. As I have explained, he will misunderstand and think you are punishing him for standing still. The time for reprimands is when he starts doing something wrong, not when he stops.

It depends on the individual horse how many times you may need to repeat this lesson before he decides that bucking is not a good way to get what he wants. Once he makes that decision, the bad habit is broken.

In essence, the bronco busters of the Old West brought that decision another way. They simply let the horse buck, giving him punishment with whip and spur at the same time, until he concluded that he could not get rid of the wrangler that way. A lot of broncs had to be "busted" all over again every time they were ridden. But if you can stay with him, it's another way—more strenuous than getting his head up—to solve the problem.

20
The Horse That Shies

For the most part, shying should not really be classified as a bad habit. It is the timid horse's natural, instinctive reaction to something that frightens him—something his senses tell him is potentially dangerous.

As discussed in earlier chapters, the horse survived as a species in the wild because nature equipped him to react to a frightening stimulus first and ask questions afterward. So there is often no valid reason for the horse to be afraid of many of the things he shies at. A fluttering piece of paper on the ground can't hurt him; a rabbit bounding across the trail is not a dangerous predator; a flapping tarpaulin on a passing truck is no real menace. But the horse does not wait to question those things. They are enough to startle him, so he shies.

To a large extent it tends to be a self-curing affliction. As a horse matures and sees more and more of the world, he tends to be less easily frightened. His experience gradually conditions him to accept the things he used to find startling. And the more confidence he has in his rider—the more security he gains from the calm, assured hand on the reins—the more readily he accepts the unfamiliar. As with many other bad habits, time and patience are the specific prescriptions for the horse that shies.

There are, however, horses who make you wonder how genuine their fear is when they shy. They are the ones who will shy at the slightest provocation while headed *away* from the barn, and completely ignore the same—or more frightening—things on the way home. If that is the kind of shyer you happen to have, you can safely bet that his fear is not as real as he would like you to believe. He is the kind that probably should draw a reprimand—a sharp

A horse shies most often because something unfamiliar scares him. By introducing unfamiliar objects in a familiar surrounding you give him a chance to learn that they are harmless.

word, a heel in the ribs, or a swat with the crop—when he shies at seemingly unreasonable things.

When in doubt, though, I prefer to give the horse an opportunity to learn first.

At one time I had a stable about a quarter of a mile from a major interstate highway. In order to get to the back roads where I liked to ride, it was necessary to get the horses through the highway underpass. I don't recall that any horse ever went directly through it the first time he was asked. It was ominous-looking at best. The sound of traffic passing overhead was downright spooky. The horses naturally did not like it.

To teach them to go through, it was always helpful to have another horse, already trained to the underpass, to lead the way. But that alone was not always enough. Some new horses would follow the leader in spite of their trepidation; others would not. My system was to ride as confidently as possible as close to the underpass as the horse would go. When the horse planted himself and refused to go farther, I let him stand and consider it for a few minutes. As long as he stood and looked warily at the entrance, I would leave him alone, just talking to him, stroking his neck, and trying to relax him.

What I would not let him do was turn away or back up. Then, if he did not make a move in a few minutes, I would squeeze with my legs and encourage him by voice. If that still did not do the trick. I would dismount, reassure him, and try to lead him through the underpass. Sometimes that worked. Occasionally he would not follow me and I, still on foot, would have to turn him around and back him through the underpass.

Two or three lessons like this almost invariably sufficed. Each time the horse experienced the frightening underpass and had the chance to learn that it was really harmless made it easier the next time.

Those who enjoy entering their horses in horse show competition can't wait for age and experience to cure their promising young prospect of the tendency to shy. So, if they want to succeed at the shows, they create all kinds of situations and obstacles at home and accustom the horse to them ahead of time. The winners in trail classes are almost invariably the horses that have been more thoroughly schooled at home. The people who do the winning don't wait until they get to the show to educate the horse.

Not all kinds of hazards can be anticipated, however. And at one show I watched a thoroughly professional trainer demonstrate what was probably a classic example of the right way to handle a flighty horse that wants to shy.

The mare he had to show was known to be alert, to say the least. She had, in fact, a reputation for being totally unpredictable. Early in the morning, before the show, I watched the trainer ride the mare into the ring. Halfway down the side of the rail she came to the officials' stand which, in this arena, was close to the rail and elevated to just about the level where anyone in it would be staring directly into the horse's eyes.

It was not surprising that the mare shied when she reached it. Shied? What she did was leap twenty feet sideways into the middle of the ring. But the trainer, giving no indication that anything unusual had happened, simply guided her around in a gentle circle, back to the rail, and approached the stand again. This time the reaction was exactly the same except that maybe the mare only jumped eighteen feet this time.

Again, staying completely calm so as not to add to the mare's

The winners in trail-horse classes at horse shows are usually the horses that have been thoroughly schooled on every kind of obstacle at home.

already ample anxiety, he brought her around again...and again...and again.

It all probably took less than half an hour. It seemed longer. But the trainer never lost his "cool" and the mare gradually seemed to find hers. Finally the moment came. She reached the officials' stand and ever so warily went by it without jumping and shying away.

At that point the trainer did what was probably the most impor-

Teaching a horse to walk over a sheet of plywood on the ground won't guarantee that he will act the same way when he comes to a real bridge. But the more confidence he develops in his rider through schooling, the better the chance he will accept the unfamiliar.

tant key action of the whole session. He *immediately* rode the mare around to the gate, dismounted, and put her away. In her class later that day, the mare went past the stand with no trouble, and she won the class.

Considering the basic psychology at work here, stopping when he did accomplished the trainer's purpose well. At first, the mare had shied out of fear. The trainer was careful not to increase the stress or her insecurity. He did not urge her or punish her. He simply and calmly brought her back to the point of decision again and again until she made the alternate choice. As soon as she did, he rewarded her. Had he asked her to repeat the right move (and pass the stand several more times) he would have introduced confusion. The mare might well have asked, "What does he want me to do?" Overschooling when you have gotten the response you want always introduces the risk of creating new tensions and insecurities that will undo the good you have accomplished.

The same point is valid whether you are breaking a horse of the habit of refusing to jump or something as simple as refusing to back. Too much schooling in one session is often worse than not enough.

21
Mixing Gaits

Mixing gaits, as opposed to breaking from one gait to another, is an annoyance to the casual rider and a serious problem to those who aspire to the show ring.

To a purist, it is technically inaccurate to speak of "mixed" gaits because a gait that is not true is actually another gait. It is easier to describe a four-beat canter as "loping in front and trotting behind." But it is technically more accurate to admit that this pattern of footfall is actually a syncopated single-foot.

The descriptions can be carried to ridiculous extremes, though. There was once a Walking Horse exhibitor who soundly criticized a judge at a show for giving a ribbon to a horse which, he said, was "pacing with his left hind foot." How a horse can do any gait with one foot, and another gait with the others, is more of a mystery than I can manage.

So, call it what you will, what we are talking about is the habit some horses acquire of getting out of the normal and correct synchronization of any gait.

I watched a tragic accident one day involving a big half-Saddlebred horse. Although he was not prime show material, he had his sire's propensity for the saddle gaits and had been taught to slow gait and rack.

Now, however, he was being schooled to become a jumper. Approaching one fence a little awkwardly, the rider tried to shift him into the right position for take-off. The signal threw the horse into a kind of mixed-up rack just before the jump. He was hopelessly discoordinated when he left the ground, and he fell on landing, breaking his neck.

Almost all horses have three gaits that they do naturally. In the large majority, these are the walk, trot, and canter. (There are distinctions in the manner of executing the lope, canter, gallop, and run, but they are all basically the same gait.) There is also a significant minority of horses that substitute a lateral gait for the diagonal trot. They do a walk, pace (or running walk) and a canter without being taught. A few horses can do more than three gaits naturally without training.

It is this last group that is probably most inclined to mix gaits under saddle. I was once asked to break a mare that was half Saddlebred and half Walking Horse. I have seen her when loose in pasture do six different gaits at one time or another. Under saddle she mostly wanted to do all six at once.

For any horse that has these tendencies, proper bitting and shoeing are particularly valuable in discouraging the habit. The rest is training.

For example, let's say the problem is a horse with a tendency to fall into an amble or single-foot when he is supposed to be trotting. Logic suggests that doing the opposite of what a trainer does when he teaches a horse to rack should be a technique to use when you want to teach him not to.

If you want to train a horse to rack, you begin with shoeing. You cut his front feet short and leave them barefoot or shod with very light plates. The hind feet, though, are left long and shod with heavy shoes. You then collect and gather the horse as much as possible, restraining with the hands while urging with your legs. For your training area you select a stretch with a slight downhill grade and firm (or even stony) footing. Giving his head a shake as you urge him, you help the horse switch from his normal diagonal gait to a lateral, side-wheeling way of moving.

The opposites are obvious: longer hoofs in front with a medium heavy shoe; shorter feet behind with lighter shoes; less collection; working uphill (or in harness with a heavier jog cart); and a light steady hand on the rein.

The lateral gaits — the pace, slow gait, amble, running walk, and rack—are more readily performed on hard footing and under light load. Standardbreds that normally trot have a tendency to drop into a pace if worked downhill at speed while those who normally pace may try to trot if the footing is soft, the inclination is uphill, or the weight of the vehicle they are pulling is increased. However, it is far easier to teach a trotter to pace than it is to teach a pacer to trot. So by the same token, it is not always easy to break a horse of the tendency to single-foot when he is supposed to be trotting.

A wide variety of shapes and types of horse shoes can be used to accomplish desired modifications in a horse's gait.

The far more common problem with mixed gaits, however, is the horse that cross-canters. While the rhythm of the gait—three beats—is the same as a true canter, the leading hind leg is the opposite from the leading front leg. In a true canter (left lead) the sequence of footfalls begins with the right hind foot, then left hind and right front striking together, followed by the left front, after which there is a period of suspension when, momentarily, none of the feet are on the ground.

The cross-canter is similar. The stride begins with the left hind foot, then the *right hind and right front* striking together, followed by the left front and a period of suspension.

Not only rougher to ride than a true canter, the cross-canter is unbalanced and in a tight turn the horse is quite likely to lose his balance and stumble.

Green colts, who sometimes don't seem to know which foot to put down next, are quite likely to cross-canter occasionally until they get the hang of juggling the extra weight of a rider on their backs. With continued work, if they are asked to canter properly, they will generally discard the habit and canter in the correct way because they learn that it is a more secure method of progression. Some regular work in small circles (either under saddle or on the lunge line) will help them to learn this lesson.

Running a horse into a gallop from a fast trot makes it a lot more likely that he will cross-canter. And the false gait turns up regularly in stock horse and dressage events where the horse is asked to make a flying change of lead. More definite application of the aids, and more precise timing in applying them, will usually correct the problem of the horse that only changes at one end.

In some horse show classes, particularly in the Western divisions, we see exaggerated versions of the normal gaits—a jog so slow that it is not a two-beat gait ("walking behind"), a four-beat lope, or lope without suspension. These variations of true gaits have been taught to the horse intentionally. They have become habitual only to the extent that the horse has practiced them a long time. But they can be untaught just as readily. They do not involve neurotic reactions.

Most other anomalies of gait such as hitching, difficulty in taking one lead, and others, may be a sign of an unsuspected lameness. An examination by the vet may reveal a cause that can be corrected.

Proper shoeing is also vital. As with any other skilled craft, horseshoeing has its artisans and its incompetents. The fact that your farrier has a sign on his truck saying "Corrective Shoeing" does not necessarily make him good at it. If the man you are using seems unable to trim the feet so they match, equips every horse with exactly the same kind of shoes, and is lacking in constructive ideas about correcting the problem you are having, it might be a good idea to ask some other horse owners to recommend someone else.

Don't expect any miracles, though, unless you understand that a horse needs to have his feet trimmed and shoes reset at intervals of four to eight weeks.

Many of the other habits we have considered develop as an escape or compensation connected with something the horse doesn't want to do. Cross-cantering and mixing gaits do not qualify under that definition. The horse gains nothing by it. So correcting it is not a question of reconditioning a neurotic response. It is just a question of teaching the horse (or the rider) the right signals and the right response to them.

22
Bad Habits in Harness

The Twentieth Century is probably the first time in all history when riding horses have a clear-cut majority over horses used in harness. Historians and archaeologists disagree on which use came first. But through most of recorded history there have been more horses pulling chariots, wagons, plows, barges, carriages, carts, gun caissons, sulkies and stagecoaches than there have been horses carrying riders.

The internal-combustion engine brought cars, trucks, buses and tractors to take over most of the heavy work and assigned the horse his present role, which is largely recreational. It is perhaps surprising to realize that there are more people riding today than at any time in history. No longer the necessity he once was, the riding horse is nevertheless more popular than ever.

Horses used for driving, though, are less numerous. In many parts of the country it is hard to find a suitable place for pleasure driving. The country roads have been paved out to the tree roots, and fast-moving traffic makes driving on the highways both dangerous and unpleasant.

Still, there are many people who enjoy driving and many trainers who praise the value of harness work in breaking colts and conditioning older horses.

In harness, a horse develops bad habits for the same reasons that he might learn them under saddle. The usual habits are the same, too: balking, rearing, kicking, running away, etc. The horse uses one escape route or another to avoid doing things that frighten him or otherwise cause discomfort. So the way that you approach correcting bad habits in harness is pretty much the same in theory. It is only in certain details that the methods differ.

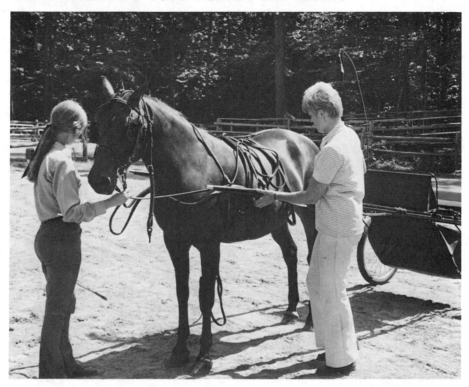

At the start, never attempt to harness a horse without an assistant to hold him while you hook him.

Driving implies harness and a vehicle, either of which may turn out to be the instrument that can frighten the horse. The only serious difficulty I have ever had with horses in harness, in fact, resulted from equipment breaking unexpectedly.

Once, in my teens, I was working a mare to a one-horse hay rake. She had been quietly plodding around the field on a lazy summer afternoon when the safety girth on the harness popped, allowing the shafts to ride up on her shoulders. It startled her and she took off, running and kicking to be free of the rattling contraption behind her.

I was quite unable to stop her and in the ensuing wild ride I fell across the shafts, got thoroughly kicked, and finally fell through into the teeth of the rake which miraculously did not stab me but lifted me like a windrow of hay and deposited me on the ground in a heap. As I landed I caught a glimpse of the mare breaking loose from the rake and heading for the barn.

When the harness is ready and the driver is in place, the assistant hooks the check rein and leads the horse forward.

In addition to the two driving reins, a safety line may be attached on one side. In case of trouble, the driver can hop out of the cart and keep control of the horse.

Twice more in later years I have been ejected from a jog cart when something broke and a green young horse took off. Those experiences—and some others when I was not dumped—have taught me that sound equipment is a must for driving any horse. An extra-stout harness and cart are in order if I have a problem horse on my hands. As long as the equipment holds up, I can ride as fast as the horse can run, and if I can stay with him, I can get him under control.

Beyond the need for sound equipment, there is a need for the right equipment. I had a mare, for instance, that was balky in harness as long as I tried to drive her in an overcheck bridle. But when I changed to a side-check bridle and eliminated the check bit, the problem went away.

A two-wheel jog cart with fixed shafts is recommended until your horse has overcome any problems with driving. It has several advantages over a four-wheel buggy. If the horse backs up, it can't jackknife. If he rears, the shafts will keep him from coming over backward (although he can fall sideways). And the simple fact that it is smaller makes it more maneuverable and less likely to create frightening problems. By all means avoid rickety, rattly old vehicles. The quieter it is the better.

There is a reason why driving bridles always come with blinkers. They direct the horse's attention straight ahead and cut off his vision to the sides and rear. Since a horse will rarely try to move in a direction he can't see, the blinders encourage him to move in the desired direction as well as keep him from being frightened by the sight of the cart behind him.

Proper adjustment of the harness is important, too. Starting at the head, the bridle should be adjusted so that the bit rests at the right place in the horse's mouth. If it is too high or too low, there will be problems. The same is true of the checkrein.

The harness saddle is placed slightly farther back from the withers than a riding saddle, and it does not need to be cinched up quite as tightly. But the safety girth that holds the shafts down should be snug.

Adjust the traces so that the points of the shafts are about even with the points of the horse's shoulders. If the shafts protrude in front, there is a chance that a rein may get caught around one if the horse swings his head to one side. Use trace extenders, if necessary, so that you can position the horse correctly in the shafts.

Some horses are irritated by breeching, and for light harness work it is not needed.

For a horse that tries to kick in harness, the specific remedy is a kicking strap. Usually a part of the breeching (which can be removed), the kicking strap passes over the horse's rear quarter, through the backstrap, with its ends fastened securely to the shafts on either side. In order for the horse to lift his feet and kick, he must then lift the whole cart off the ground.

Finally, the backstrap and crupper should be adjusted to the right length to keep the saddle from slipping forward but not tight enough to pull on the base of the tail. Some horses are upset by having their tails lifted to go through a closed crupper strap, and for them a crupper that buckles at the side can be helpful.

A generation or two ago, one of the most common ways of breaking a young horse to harness was to hook him double with a well-trained, dependable horse. In short order the older horse broke the younger one for you.

Nowadays that is not usually a convenient approach for most

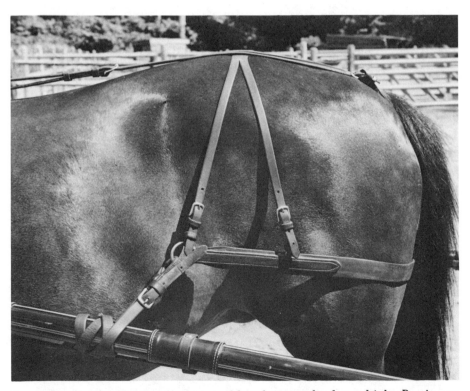

Breeching is actually designed to enable a horse to back a vehicle. But it can also help to make kicking difficult. The strap over his croup makes it impossible for him to lift both hind feet to kick without lifting the whole vehicle.

people. But it suggests some principles that can be useful. Consider that the older horse represented a source of security for the new trainee. The colt soon decided that there wasn't much to fear from the rattling trace chains, creaking harness, and rumbling wheels if his partner seemed calm about them. In the absence of a teammate, your horse needs to be introduced to those sounds and feelings gradually and allowed to get used to them while absorbing confidence and assurance from you.

If it is done properly, it can prevent trouble. I remember one young horse who was sufficiently prepared for harness work so that his complete confidence in me overcame a potentially frightening accident.

I was training a four-year-old stallion. Because he was considerably older than most colts are when they begin their training, I took more pains than usual about establishing communication with him. He seemed to learn quickly and willingly, but I made sure of his acceptance of each preliminary step before I went on to the next.

Finally, the time came when I was ready to hook him. The first day, all went well. But the next day—his second time in harness—a tire on the jog cart blew out. It made a sound that seemed louder to me than a cannon shot. Instinctively, I yelled, "Whoa!" The colt stopped dead in his tracks and stood, frightened but unmoving, while I unhooked him and led him back to the barn. I have always felt this was an outstanding example of how careful training can replace a horse's natural fear reactions with confidence in the handler.

In harness, your lines of communications with the horse are different than they are under saddle. You depend on the reins, your voice, and the whip, but you don't have the physical contact through your legs and seat.

The feel of the reins is quite different, too. Because a driving rein is much longer and broader, it weighs more than a riding rein. Until you get used to that weight, you feel as if you have a much heavier hold on the horse's mouth than you have. It takes a more positive action on your part to signal the horse with the reins. When you pull one rein to turn under saddle, your hand only needs to move an inch or two. In harness, you have to pull more than that just to take up the slack in the rein.

For people attuned to riding, there is an unfamiliar feeling, too, in the longer turning radius required in harness.

The differences are minor, but the handler needs to get used to them in order to develop the confidence and self-assurance needed to cope with a horse that has bad habits. An inexperienced driver obviously should not attempt to straighten out a horse that is difficult in harness anymore than a green rider should try to correct a horse with bad habits under saddle.

Patience and gradual introduction of new experiences will usually pay off in a horse that is cooperative and obedient in harness as well as under saddle.

Beyond the use of good equipment, careful preparation, and minor adjustments in the way you communicate with your horse, innovation and imagination are a valuable aid in dealing with problems. As I have said before, different horses have different problems for different reasons. They need to be treated individually.

By applying the rule of reason in one case, I found a simple solution. The problem was a handsome black gelding who had the habit of starting out like an explosion. When he was hooked and checked up, you needed a secure seat in the cart and a firm grip on the reins, because his first moves were always a series of wild, rearing leaps. It was not hard to bring him under control once he got that out of his system. After that he would drive very nicely. But those first fifty yards could be pretty frightening.

In harnessing, I have always followed the practice of hitching the horse before hooking up the checkrein. I do that last, when we are ready to drive off. Following this sequence usually helps to keep the horse relaxed and quiet while you are getting ready.

With this gelding I began to suspect that hooking up the check rein was his signal to explode. So I decided to try an experiment. The next time I drove him, I put the harness on in the barn as usual. But before I took him out to hook him up, I fastened the check.

He came out calmly and stood quietly while I hooked him. Then, when I got in the cart and asked him to move, the change was dramatic. He wasn't perfect. He gave one little jump first. But after several more practice sessions his problem was gone—so long as the check was hooked before he came out of the barn.

With problems in harness as well as problems anywhere else, when the method you are using is not getting results, it pays to try something different. Small changes are often all you need.

23
Preventing Bad Habits in Foals

Newborn foals begin life with no habits, good or bad. But they quickly develop attitudes and patterns of behavior that will become habits in a short time. So there are a number of things that the owner of a foal should do to help channel the youngster in desirable directions.

Until he is weaned, the most important influence in the foal's environment is, obviously, his mother. She is his source of food, his constant companion, his disciplinarian, his example and his primary source of security. Although nature has endowed most mares with a definite maternal instinct, they are by no means all alike in the way they care for their babies. Some mares are definitely better mothers than others.

Though it is not common, a few mares will reject their own foals at birth. This is most likely to happen with maiden mares having their first foals. It is a new experience to them, and some human intervention may be needed to help nature along.

If you are present when the foal is born, don't be in too much of a hurry to enter the stall of a foaling mare. The presence of intruders—even people the mare knows very well—can be upsetting at this critical time. As long as the birth is progressing normally, stay away from the mare and watch quietly from a discreet distance.

It is particularly important to let the mare smell and lick the newborn foal soon after it is born to establish recognition. There have been cases when an overly zealous owner has towelled the foal dry before the mare has had a chance to care for her own baby; as a result the mare did not recognize the foal as her own. If the mare does not establish the maternal bond in the first few minutes after birth, she may never accept the foal.

The next critical item on the agenda, after the foal has managed to get up onto his wobbly legs, is to see that he nurses successfully. He needs the colostrum that the mare secretes preceeding her true milk to give him antibodies against disease. And he needs nourishment.

Left alone, most mares and foals will work all this out very nicely by themselves. But in rare instances, most commonly with maiden mares, they do not. Occasionally the mare's udder will be swollen and sore, so that the foal's first attempts at nursing are painful to her. In these cases it may be necessary to either restrain the mare while the foal nurses or to milk the mare by hand to relieve the pressure. In this case, of course, save the colostrum in a clean container so you can give it to the foal by bottle.

Once again, don't be too anxious to help. Give nature a chance. But if the mare continues to prevent the foal from nursing by moving away whenever he tries, you may be able to solve the problem by tying her in the stall. A mare that is used to attention may feel more secure if you hold her until the foal nurses. In some cases a twitch may be necessary, or you may have to hold up one of her front feet to prevent her from kicking until she becomes comfortable with the foal nursing.

In most cases you'll only have to do this once. Occasionally it may be necessary to intervene several times until both mare and foal have settled into the routine. If the mare does not permit the foal to nurse within an hour or so, get your vet or an experienced horseman to help you without delay.

Fortunately, most mares seem to know that you are trying to help in the period just after foaling, and they tend to be quite complacent about the things you need to do for them such as removing the placenta, cleaning and rebedding the stall, and disinfecting the foal's navel. Within a few hours however, many mares begin to be very protective about their new offspring. The maternal instinct becomes very strong, and mares that are normally easy to handle may need to be approached with extra care while their foals are young.

It is helpful to both the mare and the foal in the early post natal period to provide a routine that offers as much security as possible. You want to avoid situations that the mare will consider threatening to her baby. She and the foal should be allowed to be alone for a few days. They should have a quiet stall and a private paddock, at least until the foal is able to keep up with his mother.

In general, nervous mothers tend to produce nervous babies. Foals are much inclined to copy their mothers' behavior.

One of the best brood mares that I ever had was ordinarily one of the most co-operative horses I have ever known. I can't imagine an animal being any more free of bad habits than she was. She would do just about anything you might ask of her. But her personality changed noticeably whenever she had an infant foal at her side. She continued to be pleasant and manageable as long as you did not get between her and her foal. When that happened, nothing could stop her from going to her baby and putting herself protectively between you and the foal.

She was also a mare who kept her foals on a short "tether" in the pasture. She quickly taught them not to stray too far from her. When it was necessary to separate her from her foals for short periods in order to groom her or provide medical attention, she was not difficult if you took her out of the stall and left the baby in a place she considered secure. You could take her away from her foals, but heaven help you if you took the foal away from her! She would whinny incessantly, pace the stall, and look for any opportunity to get out and go after the baby.

As an example of how mares differ, I had another good mare at about the same time who cared for her foals but also worried about her own fears and insecurities. In pasture she followed wherever the babies wanted to go, and in the barn she would try to hide behind her foals if she thought you were about to do something she didn't want you to do.

In all but the most extreme cases, the foal's mother is his prime source of security. So there are a lot of experiences the foal can be introduced to while he is still with the stabilizing effect of his dam. Foals can be halter broken in the stall and taught to lead. They can be introduced to the farrier and veterinarian. They can learn about grooming and basic handling. And they will tend to accept all these things better in an environment where their mothers are standing by, reassuring them that there is nothing to fear.

I am a firm believer in the value of handling foals and getting them used to people while they are very young. They learn from a daily routine that people are not to be feared, and they are more willing to cooperate when you begin training.

I had a brood mare a few years ago who had not had the benefit of handling when she was young. She had been turned out with her mother as a baby. After she was weaned, she was turned out with other foals. Until she was four years old, her only contact with people was occasionally to be herded into an enclosure for shots and worming. The only people she knew spent no time developing her confidence. And when they got hold of her, they usually did something she thought was rather unpleasant. Little wonder that she was extremely wary and usually hard to catch.

She improved considerably during the time I had her. But she remained hard to catch. When *she* wanted to come into the barn (usually at feeding time), you could get her if you were careful not to startle her in any way. Let one little move distract her, though, and she forgot she was hungry. It might be hours before she would settle down enough for someone to try bringing her in again.

Needless to say, she taught her foal to behave the same way. Her filly also was easily frightened and hard to catch. It took months of patient handling after she was weaned to build her confidence in people and unlearn the patterns she got from her mother's behavior.

Weaning is often the first really traumatic experience in a young foal's life. The way it is handled can make a considerable difference.

Two basic decisions must be made. One is when to wean; the other is how.

In the wild, foals usually remain with their dams for close to a full year until the mare is ready to foal again. By the end of ten or eleven months the unweaned yearlings are getting their nutrition from grazing, and what nursing they do is more habit and psychological ritual than anything else.

In domestic situations the youngster gains little of value from remaining with its dam more than four or five months. The foal should be eating solid food by that time, and the mare's milk production has probably diminished to next to nothing. The foal has also learned as much as his mother can teach him. It's time for him to be on his own.

There are cases when it may be desirable to wean the foal earlier. If the mare is in very poor health or condition, it may be best to relieve her of her nursing responsibilities. Similarly, if she is exceptionally difficult to handle and is teaching her foal to be the same way, earlier weaning may be an advantage. Some research statistics indicate that earlier weaning actually promotes growth. In one study, a group of foals weaned at two months and given special feeding were measurably larger than another group that was not weaned until the traditional time.

Two schools of thought exist on the best way to separate the foal from its mother. One approach is the gradual method. In this system the foal is separated from its dam for short periods each day which are gradually lengthened. Typically, the baby is put in the stall next to his dam at feeding time and returned after both have eaten their grain. Each week the foal stays away a little longer until finally he is not returned to his mother's stall at all.

While this gradual conditioning approach appeals to our humanitarian sense, there is no evidence that it is better for either the mare or the foal than the "cold turkey" approach. Balancing against the idea of gradual conditioning is the fact that the foal feels frustrated and insecure for a short time each day over a protracted period, while the foal that is weaned abruptly gets it over with more quickly.

Because I have not seen any advantage to the gradual method in practice, I tend to favor the clean break approach. It gives you a chance to get to know the baby—and for him to get to know you—at a time when he is eager to transfer his dependence to someone. If you make it a point to spend a little time with the foal each day during the weaning period, he will look forward to your visits and appreciate the attention you give him as well as the hay, feed and water you bring.

When I decide it is time for a foal to be weaned, I prepare another stall for the mare so I can leave the baby in the security of familiar surroundings. In many cases I will give the mare a small dose of a tranquilizer to help her over the immediate concern of leaving her baby. Then I remove the mare to the new stall, leaving the foal in the stall he is used to.

The mare should be moved to a stall where she and the foal cannot see each other and, if practical, where they cannot call to each other. The mare is immediately put on a diet of hay and water. Grain is withheld for a week to help dry up whatever milk she has left.

There will be some crying and calling from either or both of them for a few days. The foal will appreciate some extra attention to assuage his loneliness, which soon passes. Within a few days, or a week at the most, both mother and foal are usually well settled in the new routine.

I am also against the idea of putting two newly weaned foals into a stall together to keep each other company. It may keep them quieter at first, but eventually you will have to separate them. The result is that they have to be weaned all over again.

The newly weaned foal can go out in pasture with other horses, but he should be kept out of sight of his dam for at least a week. And he should not be put in the same paddock with her for at least a month, until you are sure that the last of the mare's milk is gone and both mare and weanling are fully free of their dependence on each other.

If the weanling has been halter broken—taught to lead and tie—before he is weaned, there is little more in the way of training to be done for many months. More than anything else, horses need to be allowed to be youngsters while they are growing. They need care and handling. They benefit from grooming. And they need exercise and freedom while they are developing. It is a mistake to start any serious training before the young horse is old enough to accept it.

Remember, a young horse, like a young child, has a very short attention span. If you ask him to concentrate on serious lessons beyond that span, you begin to introduce unwanted stress and set up the equation that can lead to undesirable habits. It is better in the long run to wait until the young horse is old enough to learn. There is no specific age that is right for all horses. But very few horses can absorb any serious training before they are two years old, and many will progress better and faster if they are not started until somewhat later than that.

Consistent, daily handling of a foal can do a great deal to establish his confidence in you and prevent the insecurities that cause bad habits. Moreover, by spending time with the youngster on a regular basis, you are able to spot potential bad habits before they become ingrained. That, of course, is the best time to deal with them. There is no question in my mind that the handling a foal receives in his first year of life will determine 90% of his adult behavior. If he is emotionally secure in that period, it will take a major trauma to turn him into a problem horse later.

24
In Conclusion

Throughout this book we have been emphasizing certain ideas. If you had no other experience with horses—had read no other books about riding and training—you might get the erroneous idea that most horses are timid, shrinking, fear-ridden beasts. That would be quite incorrect.

Most horses, on the contrary, are pleasant, placid, companionable animals. They are generally obedient and easy to handle. They are rather like young children. They need to be taught, directed, disciplined occasionally, and protected from some dangers. They are usually happy to cooperate in doing things you want them to.

But it is not the average horse that this book has been about. Our aim has been to take a look at the abnormal horse—the one who has developed a bad habit or behavior problem. With these horses there is a reason why they misbehave. And we have concerned ourselves with the fear and stress mechanisms that most commonly create bad habits.

Fear and the desire to achieve security are not the only motivating factors in the horse. But they are the strongest ones. They create the most difficult behavior problems, and when fear enters the picture, it supersedes all other natural impulses.

Most of the methods we have discussed have emphasized the importance of relieving your horse's fears by substituting security and confidence. Under some circumstances a horse can be made to obey and perform in spite of unresolved fears. But the better way to break a bad habit permanently is to remove its causes.

I am not suggesting that this is always easy to do. It almost invariably requires a good deal of time and patience. Even if the effort is completely successful, some horses are just not worth that much bother. With all the bad habits removed, a sow's ear is still a sow's ear.

Let us not suppose that all bad actors can be completely cured. No matter how carefully and persistently you work with them, some horses just don't fully relinquish their neurotic responses. They can be improved, perhaps, but not entirely cured of their bad habits.

In these cases, it is up to the owner to decide whether the horse's other qualities make him worth the continued annoyance...whether his habit is one you can live with, or whether it would be wiser to dispose of the horse.

I recall a much admired stallion whose record in the show ring had been sensational. He had won every honor available to his breed. But when retired to stud he had been disappointing. His average colts were inferior and his best were not half as good as he had been himself. All his life he had been difficult to handle, and the time came when he had to be considered dangerous. A difficult decision had to be made. Although the horse could have been sold—on his record—for a top price, the owner elected to have him humanely put to sleep rather than take the chance that he would endanger other people or get into a situation where he would be mistreated. It was not an easy choice—it never is. But under these particular circumstances, it was a wise and courageous move.

Most often, however, the owner faces a less drastic alternative. If he has a horse that won't drive, he can keep him for riding only. If he has a horse that won't jump, he can sell him to someone who doesn't care to jump. If he has a horse that he can't cure of nipping, he can accept an occasional pinch as the price of enjoying the things that the horse does well.

Every horse has an imperfection of one kind or another. Whether or not you decide to keep a horse depends on how much his imperfections interfere with what you want of him.

It is typical of horse owners—young ones especially, but older ones as well—that they are likely to develop a special emotional attachment to their first horse. No matter how badly that horse may act, no matter how far short it may fall from their needs or ideals, they are reluctant to part with the first horse they own.

This loyalty may be commendable, but there are times when sentiment should defer to common sense. No matter how much you *think* you love a horse, if he has a dangerous habit that you can't cure, you should give up and get rid of him. Believe it or not, you will be able to care just as much about another horse, and the time will come when you will wonder why you hesitated to unload one that was likely to hurt you.

After one experience with a problem horse, most owners are more alert when they shop for another. Even so, it is not always easy to detect bad habits in a horse before you buy him.

One of your best protections is to buy from someone you know who has had the horse long enough to have discovered any problems.

I don't recommend buying any horse the first time you see him. Give yourself an opportunity to watch him in the stall. Watch him being tacked up (better still, do it yourself) and try him not only in familiar surroundings but away from his home stable if possible.

Unless the horse you are considering is offered by someone in whom you have complete confidence, make a visit when you are not expected and see if the horse seems to respond the same way that he did when the owner knew you were coming.

By all means have the horse examined by a veterinarian before you buy. And it is not unusual to arrange to take a horse home on a trial basis. Don't think of this as an insult to the seller's veracity. There are plenty of horses that are entirely as represented by the seller but still not exactly what you want.

A few years ago, for instance, I sold a horse on a trial basis. The prospective buyers agreed that he was beautiful, but they decided not to keep him. As far as they were concerned, he was too perfectly trained. They wanted something with a little more challenge!

When you have found a horse that meets your requirements, and found him free of bad habits, the principles in this book can also help you prevent new habits.

Stress sets the stage for escape, and escape opens the route to repetition and the formation of a bad habit. To prevent that cycle, handle your horse so as to avoid or minimize stress.

With a new horse, get thoroughly acquainted with him before you begin asking him to perform. The first thing I do with any horse is to approach him in the stall. Talking quietly and moving slowly, I take his halter in one hand and gently stroke his eyelids with the other. Then I introduce myself by softly blowing my breath into his nostrils. This is an old trick that fixes my identity in the horse's mind. It won't change the way he acts, nor will it immediately give him the confidence in me that I want to develop. But he will never consider me a stranger, and, as we proceed, I will have familiarity on my side.

Index